*May al
be,
Zara*

LABYRINTHS

journeys of healing,
stories of grace

Irish petroglyph labyrinth

LABYRINTHS

journeys of healing, stories of grace

Zara Renander

Bardolf & Company
Sarasota, Florida 2011

Bardolf & Company

LABYRINTHS
journeys of healing, stories of grace

ISBN 978-0-9827918-7-5

Published by Bardolf & Company
    5430 Colewood Pl.
    Sarasota, FL 34232
    941-232-0113
    www.bardolfandcompany.com

Cover design by Shaw Creative
Cover photograph by Allison Lewis

To my grandchildren
Julia Grace, Anasara and Nora Wren

with much love and hope
that they will be people
of blessing for their generation.

Table of Contents

Acknowledgments

I am grateful to the many people who have shared their stories with me and trusted me as a companion on the Way. Without them, I would not have understood how profoundly journeys in the labyrinth can heal and ease the soul. I am also very thankful for my friend the Rev. Kerry Holder-Joffrion, who has accompanied me on so many of my travels and made possible a ministry of pilgrimage and reconciliation, which is the journey of her own heart, too. Many of the stories recounted here are her stories as well, and I am honored to be her companion on the Way. I am grateful to the Rt. Rev. Marc Andrus, Episcopal Bishop of California, for trusting and supporting my pilgrimage work and for encouraging me to rely on my instinct. He and his wife, Sheila, have been constant friends and supporters, and I honor them. I want to thank my dear children, who have humored and encouraged me, even if they did not always understand why someone they love seems intent on walking round in circles, and Arthur, my husband, who has been a stalwart supporter and is a pilgrim soul himself. And above all, thanks be to God, for the journey!

The contemporary stories related here are all true, although the names have been changed to protect confidentiality.

"Labyrinths in Stone" by Marty Kermeen

Introduction

I did not choose the labyrinth, the labyrinth chose me. I knew about labyrinths. I'd walked quite a few, including the great labyrinth at Chartres, but somehow they'd never grabbed my full attention. I liked them intuitively. I understood that there was beauty and energy surrounding them, but didn't realize that walking a labyrinth could be a transformative, life-changing experience. I had not made the connection that the life story of the walker and the physical walk itself lead to healing and blessing.

For the last few years, the labyrinth has inserted itself into my life. I have received invitations to speak about and train people in labyrinth use from both the medical and religious worlds. In doing so, I have found that people are deeply attracted to the stories surrounding the labyrinth, especially the ones that deal with healing and transformation. They want some of the theory and rationale, too, but it is the stories that provide the fizz, energy and interest to take the work of healing in the labyrinth forward. That is why I decided to interweave some of the stories I've been told with the background, history, theory and understanding of labyrinths. I hope that people who have an interest in labyrinths or have labyrinths on or near their property will find these stories helpful in imagining how their own labyrinths might be used for community healing, blessing and grace.

A number of authors have written prolifically of the history and use of labyrinths, foremost among them, the Rev. Dr. Lauren Artress of San Francisco, who in many ways is responsible for bringing the modern labyrinth consciousness to birth. My friends, Robert Ferré, Lisa Moriarty and Marty Kermeen, have built more labyrinths than they can probably remember. Jill Geoffrion has a global ministry of labyrinth use and has brought it to Myanmar, the Congo and Rwanda in order to encourage spiritual healing and strength in those troubled countries. Countless others have shared their knowledge and practice of the labyrinth.

Most of the books written about the labyrinth contain a wealth of information on how to walk one, how to make one, and various exercises and ways to use a labyrinth, but there are not many stories of what has happened to people as a result of their walk. I have been privileged to hear powerful stories of healing and reconciliation that happened as a result of a labyrinth walk. By sharing these stories, I hope to encourage labyrinth companions and facilitators to widen their imaginations and see the labyrinth as a tool for community healing. I believe these stories are an important addition to labyrinth literature.

The earliest story we have of the labyrinth comes from ancient Greece, and I was introduced to it early in my life. My father, who graduated from King's College, Cambridge, with an education in the Classics, regaled my sister and me with stories of the Greek myths. In those days, there were no TV cartoons to supplement my imagination, and I could visualize it all: Perseus battling Medusa with her hair of writhing snakes, the Greek soldiers hiding in the wooden horse before the walls of Troy, and the billowing black sails of the ship as Theseus sailed across the wine dark Aegean Sea for his encounter with the minotaur in the labyrinth on the island of Crete.

Curiously, like many people today, my father never saw these myths as anything other than thundering good stories He dismissed them as neither factual nor literally true, and therefore irrelevant, and missed their spiritual or psychological overtones, which point to inner odysseys that require every bit as much courage as any concrete exterior journey. Perhaps it was just that my father, having grown up in a pre-Freudian world, remained untouched by our intensely psychological, individualistic age, while my sister and I, when we got older, were able to understand the journeys and battles of the Perseus and Theseus as having metaphoric applications. I came to love the mysterious connection between exterior and interior journeys. Story, journey and transformation were linked deeply in my psyche. As a result, I have developed a passion for pilgrimage and for making the implicit explicit, for seeing a sacred road that allows us—in the context of history, place and external geography—to move towards healing and integration of body and spirit.

At first, as I began to walk labyrinths, I didn't appreciate the depth of what was being revealed to me. It was only in hindsight that I began to connect the dots and realize that the labyrinth provides profound opportunities of healing and transformation and that by going on a journey we may begin to move away and free ourselves from whatever spiritual block is holding us back. The very act of journeying, of being on the physical road, seems to call forth an accompanying journey of the spirit. Or perhaps it's the other way round: Sometimes our spirits demand that we move and change. We know we are stuck and must move. So we take a journey.

The labyrinth is a unique kind of pilgrimage or sacred journey, made within the confines of a circle. It is available to everyone. No matter what faith background or lack thereof they may have, the physical walk is a form of ritual that can bring reconciliation and healing for spiritual pain and fractured relationships.

Most of my knowledge of the healing power of the labyrinth has come from people who shared their stories with me and told me what the journey through a labyrinth meant for them. In hearing these tales, I realized that churches and civic organizations with labyrinths need encouragement to use them intentionally for healing and wellbeing. While many have built very beautiful labyrinths, they have rarely provided instruction on the different ways they can be walked; nor have they explored how to use them for community healing. That knowledge usually rests with one or two people, and if they leave the organization, it is lost with them. One hospital I know was given a beautiful labyrinth for its cancer center, but when the chaplain who understood how to use it was transferred to another ministry, not only was her knowledge lost, but the labyrinth itself was lost, and as far as I know has not yet been located.

I wrote this book then in part to encourage those who have labyrinths, but haven't really explored how to utilize them for community wellbeing. Because labyrinths are evocative places that reach deeply into our psyche, I have deliberately sprinkled poetry throughout the text. Poetry refreshes the spirit and speaks to the heart, not only to the mind. Poetry tells us truths about ourselves with an economy of words and centers our attention, just as stories can give us courage and new possibilities. I hope that by sharing the stories of how people have found courage and hope in a labyrinth walk, we can become more intentional about drawing on the power of labyrinths for the blessing of ourselves, our communities and the world.

Chapter One

Labyrinths

Here and there does not matter
We must be still and still moving
Into another intensity
For a further union, a deeper communion

—T.S. Eliot

Everywhere, people are walking in circles! On mountain tops, on the beaches, and even on Lower Broadway, Manhattan. They're tracing an ancient twisting, spiral pattern, walking the sinuous paths of labyrinths. In the last 30 years, new labyrinths have sprung up everywhere. They can be found in hospitals, churches and public parks. In the Twin Cities area in Minnesota where I live, labyrinths number in the hundreds!

Labyrinths come in all sorts of different sizes, from the grand 11-circuit labyrinth at Chartres to the 18-inch, stone-carved finger labyrinth in the atrium of the cathedral of San Martino at Lucca, to the hand-size labyrinths that are used in hospitals where people who are bedbound can let their fingers do the walking. Some are elegant, like Marty Kermeen's beautiful little spiral pictured at the beginning of the book.

Others are rough rocks laid out in a field, or pebbles on the beach that will be washed away by the tide. Still others are simple tracings of the circle pattern in the sand. But they all retain the unicursal path of the spiral to the center: The pattern of a journey, the journey of our existence. Around the circumference of the Chartres labyrinth are 113 "teeth" that look like cogs in a wheel. While there is discussion about their meaning, most probably these represent time expressed in a lunar cycle. This possibility gives additional richness to the pilgrimage symbolism of the path that represents our life's journey in and through time.

Cretan Labyrinth   Chartres Labyrinth

Reims labyrinth   Navajo labyrinth

All beautiful things possess an elegance that is deceptively simple, and the labyrinth is no exception. When artists pattern the design according to the patterns of nature, the resulting harmony pleases our souls. Powerful sacred spaces of all faith expressions are designed and constructed according to the proportions and templates of the natural world, so that we humans can find ourselves in them in harmonious relationship with the whole order of creation.

The great labyrinth at Chartres is based on the geometry of the Archimedean Spiral and the principles of the Golden Mean. For those interested in the sacred geometry of the labyrinth, there are many books that discuss the mathematics of the Chartres labyrinthine structure in greater depth. It is likely that the Greek knowledge of mathematics, which was retained and developed by Arabs during the Dark Ages and reintroduced into Europe prior to the Renaissance, was influential in the construction of labyrinths at Chartres and other significant locations. They became particularly important during the time of the Crusades, when the fall of Jerusalem to Saladin and the occupation of the southern parts of Europe by the Moors inhibited pilgrimages to the holy places there. As travel to Jerusalem and Compostela, Spain, the most important pilgrim destinations (besides Rome) became too dangerous, the labyrinth was used a substitute by the faithful. It had the advantage of being a much shorter, less expensive and dangerous journey, closer to home, but at heart it was understood to be a pilgrimage nonetheless.

While labyrinths have been part of the human experience for eons, during the Age of Enlightenment, they "went underground." Their use became suspect as having to do with superstition, magic and the occult, and possessing a spirituality that did not reflect the dawning scientific age. Some were deliberately destroyed, others fell into disuse, and churches no longer welcomed labyrinth pilgrims. The labyrinths that remained intact were but a quaint reminder of a time when the power of the transcendent and numinous seemed more imminent and immediate than the power of scientific fact and rational thought.

We became enamored of reason and intellectual accomplishment, as we treated the world as a laboratory using science and technology to find the answers to our profound questions. We began unlocking the secrets of the universe. Technology itself seemed a golden path, a unicursal way, that led to the "center of meaning and understanding." Miracles were brought into being with which to bless the world, but in our infatuation with the world of the scientific laboratory, we forgot that there are other kinds of knowledge. We were stepping on very holy ground, but forgot to honor it. In our dizzy exploration of the worlds of science, we became too familiar with head knowledge and became separated from the knowledge of the heart. We experienced a psychic/spiritual split which has caused us to experience alienation and separation from each other, from the earth, and from the whole created order.

And so, our deep souls are seeking reconciliation, even though we may not yet know what that means. I don't think it is an accident that knowledge of the labyrinth is surfacing now in our times as one of the ways we are trying to find our way back into balance and wholeness. It was only in 1991 that the Rev. Dr. Lauren Artress began removing the chairs that covered the labyrinth at Chartres, so she could walk this strange path outlined in the paving stones and realized this was a symbol of enormous importance—a symbol that had been hiding for centuries. She immediately brought the labyrinth to Grace Cathedral in San Francisco, which now has two major labyrinths. Many others are expanding her insight and knowledge about the labyrinth.

Jill Geoffrion, one of the most respected labyrinth guides, asks the question, in workshops, "What good is a labyrinth?" People answer that question in various ways, but usually it has to do with acknowledging a blessing. Walking the labyrinth is a way and path of blessing. The meaning of the word "blessing" is much more than the bestowing of a special favor, mercy or benefit on someone, or the experience of feelings and hopes of good fortune or well-being. It is not just a punctuation mark at the end of a worship service, or the signal to begin eating a meal, or a formal invocation of a deity at an official function. The deep significance of the word "blessing" has to do with conveying and participating in the active energy, power and vitality of the eternal One: The Creator. When Obi-wan Kenobi says to Luke Skywalker in *Star Wars*, "May the force be with you," he is offering a powerful blessing invoking and claiming the beneficent, energetic power of the universe.

Walking labyrinths can generate this energy in us. They are places of blessing, places of force transference and renewal where our own particular lives and stories are placed in a context of the universal story of birth, death and new birth, if we are willing to be open to these possibilities.

Sometimes, people ask me the question, "Where does the labyrinth come from, where did it begin?" While there is no definitive answer, we can say that labyrinths are a gift to us from the heart of the Creator, sacred symbols and signs pointing to a greater reality beyond ourselves. The form of the labyrinth is archetypal, present in our collective psyches, and it is now emerging once again from a deep, subconscious place in humanity's self-understanding. Story and myth bear witness to the human fascination with this ancient symbol across the globe, across cultures and across time. We have petroglyph labyrinths from Galicia, Syrian pottery shards, and ancient labyrinthine forms expressed in Navajo basket weaving. The whorls of the Nautilus seashell also mirror this design, anchored in the cosmos and the turning of the earth, a variation of which is the path of the labyrinth. For people of faith, this form is part of our spiritual heritage, a gift to assist us in locating our center, in finding our way home. For the Jesuit philosopher and theologian, Teilhard de Chardin, the spiral was a symbol of the generating energy of the universe, the Christ, the Omega Point, pulling all creation into itself, in the same way as the ball in roulette circles in a descending spiral to the center of the wheel.

Circles are symbols of inclusion and exclusion. A wedding ring is an example of a circle that is closed. It reflects and signifies a connection between two people that is protected by clear boundaries and allows no ingress or egress of others into the intimacy of the marriage relationship. The labyrinth, on the other hand, is not a closed circle, and that is one of its joys. While maintaining its clear definition and boundaries, it is also open, allowing both access and a way out.

John O'Donohue in his book *Eternal Echoes*, has this to say about the importance of the circle:

> *The one who dreamed the universe loved circles. There is some strange way in which everything that goes forward is somehow still travelling within the embrace of the circle. Longing and belonging are fused within the circle. The day, the year, the ocean's way, the light, the water, and the life insist on moving in the rhythm of the circle.*

As the great winds sweep across the earth following the path of the circle, as the tides ebb and flow at the calling of the moon, as the seasons move in a sacred circle of spring with new birth, summer of life, and fall and harvest leading to winter and death, our own spirits are called to pay attention to dance in this circular movement as well acknowledging the different energies each revolution brings, encouraging and partnering one another on the way of this sacred dance. Black Elk, the famous medicine man of the Lakota nation, noted that, "Everything sacred moves in a circle."

The open circle reflects reality as an open system, allowing space for revelation and movement that comes from deep within. The one who "dreamed the universe" into being is like a mother and we, her children following that pattern, must also give birth. As we partake of blessing, so we must also give birth to blessing around us. We who walk the labyrinth receive blessing and share blessing with others. We have the choice to live our lives intentionally, growing in awareness, walking ever deeper into the meaning of our full humanity, or we can spend our time with trivialities, shopping and entertainment. The open labyrinth points to the belief or hope that, in following the path of our lives, we can find meaning. We are not alone, trapped in a three- or even four-dimensional universe. A mystical, transcendent dimension is also part of our experience. As the child longs for the mother and the mother for the child, there is a way of connection open to us. We are not condemned to hopeless longing.

Many of us sense intuitively that we have lost our way home. We feel a spiritual isolation from one another and the Earth. Our bridges of connection and belonging seem severed, so we are out of balance with our surroundings. A child in the night, fearful of the dark and hungry, cries for its mother, for food and comfort. The mother hears and comes to her child. Paul Tillich, the theologian, imaged our spiritual longing for the Holy, the Divine, in the same way that our physical being thirsts for and needs water. He did not believe that we would possess this thirst and longing for connection if it were not possible to achieve it and if the pathways to reach it were not present. In religious terms, that way of communication is prayer in its many forms and expressions. As we long for a homecoming and re-connection with the mystical and Holy, our spirits may turn to labyrinth walks. In doing so, we engage in physical, embodied prayer and participate in the creative spiritual force of the universe.

Walking the labyrinth provides a balance in prayer form and numinous experience different from the predominantly masculine expressions that have defined of our Western spirituality. The circle itself is a feminine symbol. Too often our Western prayer forms tend towards being intellectual, heady and wordy. However, from ancient times and deep antiquity, people have prayed by dancing or walking in circles. Native Americans see all creation existing within a sacred hoop. In Celtic spirituality, a holy place, sacred well, stone cairn or shrine must be encircled seven times in prayer, an act that is very reminiscent of walking a labyrinth. The army of Israelites besieging Jericho had to march around the walls of the city for seven days. Is this pattern beginning to look familiar? The Mandala has been used for millennia as a circular prayer and geometric form of reflection. It is a representation of the universe within a circle, and is used ritually for meditation and prayer. Tactile prayer beads, the rosary, are yet another form of circular prayer, as is, of course, the finger labyrinth.

Yes, we humans have prayed and walked in circles since the dawn of our consciousness, and the renewal in labyrinth interest and use is a sign of our need to reconnect once again with this old wisdom and spiritual practice.

Chapter Two

Walking a Labyrinth

Where we thought to travel outward, we will come to the center of our own existence. And where we had thought to be alone, we will be with all the world.

— Joseph Campbell

There are many ways to walk a labyrinth: Children in Africa can do it on their hands! A walk may be a life-changing transformation, a quiet meditation, or simply an opportunity to press the reset button on our lives. For some, it is a chance to see the dark side of the moon, the aspect of their lives and behavior that causes grief and suffering, but whose cause is hidden for the moment. Two sides of a coin are revealed at the same time: The external, physical journey step by step illuminates our interior life, making the implicit explicit, creating a powerful resonance and revelation between inner and outer realities. Some dismiss the idea of the labyrinth as pilgrimage, thinking that the actual physical distance is too short to make that claim. However, the walk is never just about the geographic distance covered from point A to B, as it encompasses the spiritual depths that are plumbed.

A labyrinth is formed by a single path that leads in a spiral-like fashion to the center of a circle and out again. Unlike a maze, it has no dead ends or traps. Historically, the words "maze" and "labyrinth" have been used interchangeably, which causes much confusion, but in modern English usage an important distinction is now beginning to be made between the two different and distinct patterns. A maze is intentionally confusing and meant to trick the walker. It involves finding a path to the center and back out again, but it is easy to get lost along the way. A walk in a maze is about the art of learning the way out. It requires memory and a determination not to give up too easily. It requires making polarized judgment calls, decisions on which way to go when the path diverges. A maze walk, like the labyrinth, also may reflect aspects of our life, but it mirrors our need to solve problems and find the right way out of our dilemmas and confusion. It involves memory and recall, engages the intellect, and perhaps appeals to our sense of fun, playfulness and trickery. It is the diametrical opposite of a deeply meditative labyrinth walk, in which no problem-solving skills are required.

A labyrinth has switchbacks and turns, but there are no dead ends or traps. Walking it does not demand intellectual prowess, but draws on body-based wisdom, intuition and emotional, intelligence. There is no element of deception; there is absolute clarity about the way in and out. The only requirement is to stay on the path! That simple instruction is surprisingly difficult for most of us to follow, because it requires us to be totally present in the NOW, giving up control and allowing the way itself to lead us. The experience of the walk itself can override the intellectual demands for knowledge. In the process, it mirrors in some fashion our own life's journey with its many twists and switchbacks, revealing our interior blocks and obstructions. Instead of being asked to solve the way out, as in a maze, we are asked to trust that the path of life is made for our blessing and that it will lead us to where we need to be, and as we walk it, to be aware of both our interior and exterior realities. Easier to say than to actually do!

The traditional layout of the labyrinth corresponds to the four directions, North, East, South and West. The entrance is usually in the West so one enters facing East and the rising sun, the place of new birth. It is helpful during a walk to remember the directions and think about how they have affected you. A chaplain friend of mine had never paid attention to them until he walked with me and focused on them. He told me afterwards that he realized that most of the positive energy and blessings in his life came from the North. I have lived a great deal in a cold, northern climate, so I tend to see the South as the place of blessing and flowers. But for each walker it's a different experience, and every walk is a different walk.

Before embarking on a labyrinth walk, it is usual to remove one's shoes. On entering the labyrinth, it's important to stop for a few seconds and acknowledge that we are passing from one space to another, that we are crossing a sacred threshold. There are echoes here of God's instruction to Moses on Mount Horeb to remove his shoes, because the ground on which he stood was holy ground. On a canvas labyrinth, there is the very practical reason of not wanting to dirty it with muddy footprints. When people need to have their shoes on to walk, the facility offering a labyrinth to the public usually provides overshoes.

One traditional approach to labyrinth walking is to see the journey in three parts—the three Rs:

1. **The Way of <u>R</u>elease** leading into the center is also known as the Way of Purgation (in medieval terms). It is the journey of letting go and allowing ourselves to experience the walk.

2. **The Place of <u>R</u>eceiving** is the center itself, also known as the Place of Illumination.

3. **The Way of <u>R</u>eturn** or Way of Integration refers to the journey home as we come back to our ordinary life.

Sometimes people ask how they should walk. There's no right answer, other than to follow the promptings of your own body. You might feel the need to dance or to walk meditatively and slowly. Children frequently run the labyrinth. Do whatever feels right. Don't worry about motives or reasons. Some people walk to clear their mind, some walk for others, some for thanksgiving, others in grief. It's good to experiment and open ourselves to a wide range of possibilities.

Many books have been written about the different ways to use, pray and meditate on the labyrinth. Many of them mirror the deep spiritual/physical journey of birth, death and rebirth, or resurrected life with which all creation engages.

Often a walk will proceed simply with no great insights offered. It may just be a time allowing us to be quiet and thoughtful. However, even these walks can set up vibrations in us that are worthy of our notice. Pay attention to dreams you may have following a walk, to any synchronistic experience, like an unexpected meeting or phone call. The labyrinth calls us to be mindful on our life's journey, so be curious about what happens or does not happen afterward.

As you walk, you may experience a feeling of resistance, perhaps to others on the path, perhaps to the path itself, perhaps to some exterior stimuli, such as the noise of children playing or the sound of traffic nearby. Take time to examine these. They usually point to the place where growth can occur. How we face the challenges of life, particularly our resistances, determines how we grow into a full human being. Confronting resistance encourages us to develop spiritual muscles and greater awareness. It is one of the ways we create meaning for our existence.

The labyrinth is one of those most powerful symbols that negates itself. It implies both birth and death and, by implication, rebirth or profound change. The cross is another such symbol, as is the circle of the Tao. Sometimes people will sense this innate symbolic power and resist walking, because they intuit that entering on this circular way may transform them.

Kerry Holder-Joffrion tells of a man who held a labyrinth gathering at his house one evening. The labyrinth was drawn in lime on the lawn and he told guests that he'd let the neighbors know that they were searching for his wife's lost diamond earring! Fear of looking foolish and being exposed to embarrassment while walking around in circles is very real. A man I know who has helped me conduct labyrinth walks numerous times refuses to walk himself. He senses that the walk will demand changes in him that he's not yet ready to make. Anyone who works with the labyrinth must be sensitive to such resistance, which can take many forms.

Another expression of resistance is how we relate to others on the labyrinth with us. If someone is walking behind you, and you sense that they want to pass, it is customary to just step aside and let the other person pass. However, the issue of meeting others on the labyrinth is part of the walk, and how we encounter them is part of the experience. Many people find that they become extremely irritated by the presence of others who may seem to present obstacles and an intrusion into an individual's private prayer space. This is a resistance that is worth exploring: What is it about other people on the labyrinth that is upsetting? It raises the issue of individualism vs. community. In our Western world, we prize individualism and self-reliance, and approach most activities and endeavors with a self-centered attitude. As a result, we have trouble seeing the community dimension of labyrinths walks and pilgrimages. One couple I know decided to build a lovely labyrinth in their own garden. They laid it out in such a way that it was impossible to meet anyone else on the path. What a sign of our isolation and insistence on our individuality at the expense of relationships and community.

We have a great deal to learn from our brothers and sisters in Africa about the community dimension of the labyrinth. There is a wonderful photograph of a group of African Baptist Pastors who were working with Jill Geoffrion. They were lined up close together on the labyrinth; if one moved, they all had to move. The picture suggests a community dance and is an image of our close relationship with one another. The image also illuminates a radical understanding of prayer: What we do—how we walk and act—affects our neighbor. When we are closely aligned with our neighbors in the labyrinth, so that we have to move when they do, we experience our interdependence and are united. In this way, we are both individually and communally transformed—that concept quickly becomes a reality. One walker in South Africa remarked that if all the people of his village weren't there, he couldn't enter the labyrinth. He was expressing the classic Bantu idea of *Ubuntu*: I am what I am because of who we all are. All or nothing!

In contrast, I've heard many Americans comment that they initially get bothered and irritated by having other people on the path who become obstructions slowing them down—they don't realize that the others are part of the journey, too. This would not happen in other parts of the world, where the other is welcomed. Father Frank Fahey of Ballintubber Abbey, County Mayo, Ireland, has worked with pilgrims for many years and introduced the ancient Tochar Phadraig (the pilgrimage to Croag Patrick) to modern pilgrims. He offers this advice, which he dispenses with a great, impish smile:

- Look after one another.

- Give thanks always, even when you're miserable, cold and uncomfortable, even when you can't imagine why you're on the road (or walking in circles on a labyrinth). Say, "Thanks be to God!" and keep going.

- Go out with the intention of being transformed—pilgrimage is not tourism!

A friend who escorted a group on a pilgrimage to the Orthodox monasteries of Eastern Europe, told me about one couple that was so focused on the minutia of the trip that they completely missed the spiritual aspects of the places they visited. They spent the whole time concerned about historical facts, dates, distances and photo ops so they could fill their scrapbook to show friends back home. Unable or unwilling to relinquish control and give themselves over to the journey, they never experienced that liminal space where we cross the threshold to a different way of knowing. They never felt the movements of pilgrimage mirroring the deep spiritual/physical journey of birth, death and rebirth—resurrected life with which all creation engages.

In remarkable contrast, Jill Geoffrion, working with children in a war-torn part of Africa in the shadow of a battle, constructed a labyrinth of discarded shell casings with their help. As guns blasted away in the distance, they all prayed and walked for peace, focusing on the sacred space they had created. Like the children, we too can walk for peace in the world and in our lives. We can walk for the blessing of the world.

Chapter Three

The Story of Theseus

I give you the end of golden string
Only wind it into a ball
It will lead you in at Heaven's gate
Built in Jerusalem's wall.

—William Blake

The most ancient story we have of the labyrinth, a shard from the distant past, is the myth of Theseus and Ariadne. Some of us first heard it in grade school, others had to read it in high school. Nowadays you can find it in various books and on the Internet. Living as we do in a scientific age, most people dismiss it as an improbable, fanciful story that has no relevance today. We ignore its deep wisdom and its power to speak to our own troubled times and our own life experiences. But for those who are willing to listen carefully, it can reveal important aspects of our individual development and to comment on matters that concern all of us at this moment in history.

The basic story line that I know is as follows:

A terrible Minotaur—half bull, half man—lived in
the island of Crete. This Minotaur was the product
of a sexual union between Pasiphaë, the queen, and
a white bull that had been given to her husband,
King Minos, by Poseidon, the sea god. Minos had
received instructions from Poseidon to sacrifice the
bull, but greed got the better of him. Wanting to keep
the beautiful bull for himself, he substituted another,
lesser bull from his herd as a sacrifice, hoping the
switch would go unnoticed. But Poseidon was no
fool. His revenge was to make Queen Pasiphaë fall
in love with the white bull. Driven mad with desire,
she commissioned Daedalus, the king's engineer, to
construct a wooden cow, in which hidden from view,
she could have sexual intercourse with her beloved
white bull! The child from this unlikely union, in such an
unlikely fashion, was the Minotaur—half bull, half man.

To hide his wife's sexual deviance and shame, and
perhaps his own shame, Minos asked Daedalus to build
a labyrinth in whose deep and dark interior they could
trap the Minotaur. Perhaps Minos was not willing to kill
the Minotaur outright. Perhaps he was learning that it is
not a good idea to insult the gods! So Daedalus built
a labyrinth in the royal palace. However, as a condition
of entering the labyrinth, the Minotaur demanded
that seven young men and seven young maidens be
fed to him every year. The king acquiesced, but the
Minotaur's demand ravaged the island of Crete, to the
great distress of its citizens.

The arrangement was clearly not very satisfactory,
but deliverance arrived when there was a war with the state
of Athens. When the Minoans were victorious, King
Minos exacted an annual tribute of seven young men and
maidens. So it was that Athenian youths were sent each

year to the palace at Knossos in Crete to meet their death at the hands of the Minotaur in the labyrinth.

Not surprisingly, the Athenians deeply resented this practice, but they felt helpless to do anything about it. Finally, after three years, Theseus, the king's son, spoke up and offered to go to Crete as one of the hostages with the intention of killing the Minotaur and putting an end to the gruesome practice. The king applauded his son's courage, but he believed he would never see him again.

So the terrible day came when the hostages, with Theseus among them, were ready to sail to Crete. The crowds on the dock, who had come to say good bye, were dressed in mourning. As the victims boarded the ship, funeral dirges played. Everyone wept watching the boat with billowing black sails cast off and head towards Crete and death.

When the Athenians arrived at the dock in Knossos, Crete, it was a quite different scene. People were dancing, wearing garlands of flowers. There was music and entertainment. The princess, Ariadne, had come to see the festivities herself. Everyone was celebrating the arrival of the hostages who would satiate the Minotaur's appetite for another year.

When Ariadne saw the handsome Theseus step off the boat, she instantly fell in love. Deciding that he was far too good looking to be eaten by the Minotaur, she went to see Daedalus and asked him for advice. Daedalus told her to give Theseus a ball of golden twine. She would hold one end of the string and he would hold the other as he entered the pitch black labyrinth. If he survived the Minotaur, the string would allow him to find his way back in the darkness. Ariadne, being a resourceful woman, not only gave

Theseus the string, but also a bright sword, which he hid under his cloak.

As he descended into the labyrinth, all light faded. Theseus felt his way along the walls to orient himself in the terrifying blackness. He listened for sounds that would give him a clue where the Minotaur was waiting for him, but the beast came roaring at him without warning, and a terrible battle ensued in the center of the labyrinth. Eventually, Theseus managed to grab a hold of the Minotaur's horns. Pulling up the beast's head, he plunged the sword into his exposed chest. The Minotaur died in the labyrinth. With Adriane's string to guide him, Theseus dragged the carcass out of the labyrinth into the light of day, so everyone could see that the Minotaur was really dead. Ariadne was waiting for him at the mouth of the labyrinth. As Theseus emerged, the celebrations commenced. He and Ariadne were married and sailed away to another adventure, which did not have such a happy ending, when Theseus abandoned his bride on the island of Naxos. But that's another story.

It's worth taking time to look at this powerful ancient tale with care and examine what the various characters and their actions symbolize and how they may speak to us today.

The repercussions of this sorry tale of cupidity, sexual deviance and fraud are not limited to the participants in the royal household, but affect the whole community. Everyone suffers because of the king and queen's transgressions. The whole land is held hostage to evil.

The Minotaur, a monstrous hybrid—half human, half beast—symbolizes the animalistic, lustful and voracious side of humanity. It is significant that it has to be hidden away, because it also represents the shame of the queen's illicit sexual affair with the sacred bull and the king's greed, deception and disobedience to a god's instructions

Characteristics of shame are the desire to hide and to surround the reprehensible act with silence. People who are ashamed drop their eyes, sometimes even shutting them, so that others cannot see too deeply into their pain. With silence and denial affecting the court of Minos, the kingdom was under a permanent cloud. The victims of the Minotaur, the young men and maidens, represent the future of the community that was being devoured by a monster.

So, let's ask ourselves, both communally and individually, of what are we ashamed? What are the things we dare not speak of? What are our unspoken family secrets? What is eating our own future, as a world, as a nation, as a community and individually, and holding us hostage because we dare not mention it or confront it? What about addictive behaviors? Drug and child abuse? Deep deprivation that leads to depression and eating disorders? All the ills that affect our modern society which we prefer to ignore, hoping that they will go away.

In order to free the community and restore the well-being of Athens, Theseus has to name the problem publicly and have the willingness and courage to confront the symbol of shame, the Minotaur, directly. To succeed, he first needs the consent and blessing of the king, his father, for the undertaking. Then he receives a combination of feminine and masculine support—Ariadne represents the female, intuitive aspects, while Daedalus stands for all that's male, rational and logical. Although Theseus heads into the darkness alone, he doesn't go entirely unaided: He has the support and blessing of the community. As he descends into the terrible blackness of the labyrinth, he also holds the golden string of love which connects him to Ariadne and the outside world, and with which he can find his way back. The sword with which Theseus kills the Minotaur is the sword of truth that cuts through the deception, lies and confusion that hold us captive.

As we confront the challenges of our lives, this story provides an important model. When we engage our own Minotaurs and monsters, we must recognize and name the destructive forces that lay waste our potential and our future. To succeed, we will need the support and blessing of others. We will have to use both the sacred masculine and feminine energies and call on our own courage and determination. And if we remember to hold on to the golden thread of love, we will never sink so far into the pit of despair that we cannot return from profound darkness. When we do dare to make this journey and confront our deepest fears, which hold the future hostage, the blessing we gain is not just an individual experience. It is for everyone. The whole community benefits.

Interestingly, not only the Athenians benefited, but their enemies, too, as King Minos and the people of Crete were freed from the monster as well. Truly, when we engage in confronting our fear and that which holds us captive, the blessings extend in a veritable tidal wave over the world. When someone confronts their addictive, destructive, abusive behaviors, changing their pattern of dealing with spiritual pain, the whole community around them breathes a sigh of relief as new healthy patterns of relationship are opened up for everyone. There's nothing like a wedding, and a royal one at that, to symbolize a new future and new beginning, and in Crete the wedding celebration of Theseus and Ariadne reconciled warring states and opened the possibility of a time of peace and harmony.

Interestingly, one ancient description of labyrinths calls them Ariadne's dancing grounds, and labyrinths have certainly been used for dancing. In Auxerre, France, there is a tradition that on Easter Eve, the Dean of the Cathedral and the Bishop would enter the labyrinth with a ball of twine which they would toss back and forth as they danced into the center. Along the way, they were surrounded by the officials of the Cathedral, priests, monks, the choir and officials who sang Easter resurrection hymns. Unfortunately, while we have records that this happened, the steps of the dance and the liturgy are lost. The coming of the Age of Reason put an end to such "foolishness," but we can always develop our own dances as we celebrate new life given after confrontation with fear.

Chapter Four

The Labyrinth & Stories

A story is like water
that you heat for your bath.
It takes messages between the fire
and your skin. It lets them meet,
and it cleans you!

—Rumi

Since ancient times, human beings have sat around fires and gazed at the stars as story tellers wove epics of great hunts and acts of courage and cowardice, of times of scarcity and abundance, of peace and war. The words "Once upon a time" or "Far away and long ago" immediately open our psychic and spiritual awareness to the worlds of possibility, myth, mystery, tragedy and comedy. Sacred dances, drama and music embody the wisdom of the human race in their narrative structure and content. It can be argued that it is our ability to carry out the creative act of storytelling in its multi-faceted dimensions that makes us human beings. Today, in the reductionist world of 21st century cyberspace, we tend to share our experiences in blogs and bytes, but we're still engaged in telling stories.

Stories can reveal to us who we are and who we are not. Whether they are frivolous or sad, fact or fiction, myth or mystery, stories are powerful means of creating meaning. We human beings have a great need to make sense of our existence and time on this earth—it is a core necessity for us. Stories are vehicles that allow us to create significance and identity for ourselves and our environment. Their liminal characteristics can help us cross psychic thresholds and impart understanding of who we were, who we are and who we might become.

We have stories we tell ourselves endlessly, and there are stories that others tell or have told about us. These stories can be helpful or destructive. A relative who always describes a child as "chubby" is setting up a story of "I'm fat, and I've always been fat." Likewise, the comment in childhood that "Paul is very artistic" will have an ongoing impact, even if Paul decides to be an accountant, and it can become a story for Paul to tell about himself at some point in his life, if he chooses to do so. We all carry around in our heads narratives of ourselves, like mini-tape recordings, to which we listen daily. We have dominant stories and also secondary tales. The former usually drown out the latter, which we remember only dimly, but which impact our lives just as powerfully. These stories, conditioned by our history, our culture with its taboos, and our family and life experiences, help define reality for us. Our dominant stories often tell us who we are and what we do: I am a woman, a man, a gay person, a banker, a plumber, a farmer, etc. Our secondary tales affect the quality of our lives, often below the threshold of our conscious awareness. They can support our aspirations or hold us captive, reflecting negatively on our abilities—I'm not an accomplished speaker (Moses); I am too young (Jeremiah); I'm unworthy and I live with unworthy people in a corrupt culture (Isaiah)—and providing every excuse imaginable for failing to engage our life at its core.

We limit our potential by telling ourselves stories of disempowerment, and we gain courage when we remember that we are not defined by one particular tale. We act in accordance with the dictates of our self-told narratives and often allow ourselves and our lives to become trapped like flies in amber. However, one of our most powerful human attributes is that we are able to turn the page, alter the narrative—change the direction and outcome of the stories—and in so doing, change our lives.

Entering profoundly into a story is akin to entering a refining fire. When we examine its various levels and allow it to speak into our lives, we let the tale ask questions of us. In this sensitive, searching interplay of narrative and questioning, we may see our own life story differently and begin to tell another tale. Travelers on the labyrinth and on a pilgrim journey who allow themselves to listen to resonances of the positive secondary stories in their lives return changed and transformed. They have crossed the threshold into a country of sacred imagination, where they are able to open themselves to new dimensions and possibilities and engage in the transformative act of telling themselves a new story.

I didn't understand that the beauty and elegant form of the labyrinth could effect such profound changes until my friend and associate, The Rev. Kerry Holder-Joffrion, started to use it with a group of sexually abused girls. The National Children's Advocacy Center's (NCAC) headquarters is in Huntsville, Alabama, where Kerry is an Episcopal priest, and where I was working for a time as director of a Center for

Pilgrimage and Reconciliation. An NCAC counselor, who was also a parishioner, came to Kerry lamenting the fact that a whole year of therapy using all the right protocols and resiliency training for sexual abuse survivors did not go deep enough to reach the traumatized spirit of the child. She wondered whether Kerry could help with some ritual that might bring deep healing to these young, troubled souls. After some thought, Kerry decided to use the labyrinth, because as a sacramental place, it is an icon or window into a deeper and more profound reality.

The labyrinth also has the unique quality of belonging to the whole world and is not being owned by any religious denomination. Therefore, NCAC could keep its Federal funding while using a sacramental tool for spiritual healing.

Kerry designed a process that included a morning of background work followed by a labyrinth walk. During the morning, the girls were given a heavy rock that had been hewn out of a mountain by slaves many years ago. They were asked to paint some symbol representing an aspect of their abuse and oppression on it. One of them painted a heart that was shattered like glass. The girls were then told that they could choose to carry this weight with them into the labyrinth and, if they were ready to do so, put it down. It's important that we only put down the burdens we carry when we are willing to do so. The girls who might not be ready to do so were told to keep the stone with them as a physical reminder of abuse, and to relieve themselves of it when they felt ready. At that point, they might throw it in a river or leave it on a mountain. In fact, each girl put down her stone on the path of the labyrinth that day.

NCAC keeps excellent records, and when the counselors tabulated the evaluations by the teenagers of their experiences at the center, they were stunned. Over the course of a year of the most intensive therapy, the children considered their day in the labyrinth the most important part of their healing.

One wrote that she had had low self-esteem, was depressed and hated school. Then she described herself as "awesome—I have better self esteem." Another wrote that she had been "closed up, scared, shattered, cold, depressed." After the experience in the labyrinth, she described herself as "open, alive, strong, brave and happy." A third wrote, "Thank you for giving me back my femininity." Yet another wrote, "I realized I am entitled to be happy." The children were beginning to tell new stories about themselves, discovering new dimensions of who they were and could become.

In working with the sexually abused children, we never denied their story or its destructive power, but opened doors to other narratives. What the children were doing very effectively in their labyrinth journey was engaging in the powerful, creative act of changing their reality by changing their story. They no longer identified themselves only as "victims," with all the imprisoning, life-destructive attributes that accepting such a label entails, and they were able to accept that their sexual abuse history no longer defined them. It was part of their history, certainly, but it was not their life. The chapter on sexual abuse was only part of their story, not the whole tale. The children could see themselves differently now and could relate how they came out of this dark time as stronger and victorious survivors. They imagined a new future for themselves as agents in their own destiny.

Cancer, sickness, childhood abuse, alcoholism, AIDS, drug addiction and any other of life's vicissitudes and conditions do not have to define the core of our existence: We are not a disability we may have. We have choice in how we will confront life's challenges and what stories we tell ourselves and the world around us.

From this remarkable beginning, the counselors realized that if the labyrinth was so helpful to the children, it could be helpful to many others. As word got out, we began to receive invitations from all over the South to hold workshops and introduce the labyrinth for healing in other places of brokenness and pain. As we conducted these workshops, the people who walked the labyrinths taught us what we know, broadening our appreciation and knowledge of the transformation that was possible. They told us their stories, and how walking and praying had helped them. We listened, observed and walked ourselves; and we read to learn more from the many wise people who have been building, painting and using labyrinths far longer than we had. During our presentations about the labyrinth and healing, we came to realize how important stories were to the process.

Over the last few decades, the work of Michael Wright and David Epston has opened up a new world of storytelling as a reconciling and transformative approach. Narrative Therapy has become an valuable tool in helping people understand the stories that have shaped them, often in oppressive and destructive ways, and recognize that there is no one, determining voice or story in our lives. In Latin and South America, the work of Paolo Freire helped indigenous people name their social, political and economic oppressions, tell their own stories and claim their own identity, which in turn led to a movement for land reform. In South Africa, the Rev. Michael Lapsley has used the power of storytelling with journey and ritual to heal and transform those who were deeply traumatized by the evils, violence and brutality of apartheid.

43

The sacred art of storytelling can build bridges of meaning, reconciliation and new possibility, so we may journey from a static, oppressive, one-dimensional narrative to one that is liberating and multi-faceted.

As the power of story to change lives and make whole again became apparent to us in our work, we also realized that linking it with ritual enhances the process dramatically because ritual is embodied story.

In Selma, Alabama, some 40 years after the Civil Rights struggle, Kerry and I were invited to help the vestry of St. Paul's Episcopal Church face involvement in the dark story of racial segregation. Of course, most of the original parishioners of that era were either dead or no longer living in the area. We were dealing with an inherited story, which can be every bit as powerful as an individual's personal narrative. When we asked people to tell the story of their family's participation in the history of segregation, we were met initially with polite stonewalling. After we managed to build a bit of trust, the stories came tumbling out. One man brought his White Citizen pin, a badge of his coming into manhood, saying, "I don't know why I brought it today, but I did." He put it down on the circles of the labyrinth, saying he would never pick it up again. He was ritualizing his rejection of that part of his story. He also told of his father, who had been one of the members of the riot police posted at the other end of the Edmund Pettus bridge during the march led by the Rev. Martin Luther King, which culminated in frightful violence 40 years earlier. He said that his father, who was not a bad man, knew things had to change, but didn't know how.

During the meeting, as tears began to fall, we heard an important and interesting comment, "This is the first time anyone has asked us to tell our stories. We've heard the stories of the Black community, but no one asked for ours. Thank you!" Later, we were invited to walk the Pettus Bridge with the vestry of St. Paul's, including the man whose father had been a policeman, who accompanied a young African American teenager, and told the story of his father's participation in the march. Physically crossing the bridge together, engaging in sacred pilgrimage and telling stories brought healing and wholeness. Today, St. Paul's Church works with Brown Chapel to help feed the pilgrims, black and white, who come each year to cross the bridge. Today, they walk together.

As we welcome home men and women who have fought for our country and who find it difficult to adjust to conditions outside the theaters of war, where battle conditions and violence become ingrained as daily routine, intentional use of stories and ritual in the labyrinth is a powerful way to help them reenter their former lives. It allows them to reconnect with themselves and their families, and to deal with the stress of incorporating their experiences into a place of acceptance and reconciliation. I believe that this is deeply important and necessary, and that the labyrinth has a place in this work.

The need for such soul work is great and reaches far beyond our borders. In Myanmar, Rwanda, and the Congo, Jill Geoffrion has been working with groups that have suffered genocide and extreme political oppression, offering to restore wholeness by and releasing their terrible history in the labyrinth. Rather than life remaining "A tale told by an idiot, full of sound and fury, signifying nothing," as Shakespeare's Macbeth called it after he had turned the struggle with his enemies into a horrific bloodbath, they can find meaning and grace with a new world open before them.

Across the country, we have many labyrinths. The next stage is training people in how to use them for blessing and new life in the communities in which we live. From the ashes of Ground Zero to the Gulf shores devastated by Katrina and the BP oil spill; from the person facing a journey with cancer as an uninvited companion to a young child dealing with sexual abuse, and to the veterans and their families looking to find a new way of coming together after returning from a war zone, the labyrinth silently offers hope and a path to new beginnings.

Chapter Five

Crossing Thresholds

Leaving the old, both worlds at once they view,
That stand upon the threshold of the new.

—Edmund Waller

For most of our lives, we live within the humdrum and known boundaries of a familiar world. But just sometimes, the soul responds to a longing, a call from the borderlands, from beyond the known and safe parameters of our days. It is when we are way outside of our comfort zones, stripped of the familiar "props" of our lives, that our souls begin to breathe and grow again. Then we are in touch with what we didn't know that we knew, with the reservoir of wisdom that lies dormant and hidden in the great silence and shadows within us. So we begin to restore a balance that we have lost in the routine of our day-to-day existence.

Each day is a new beginning of darkness and light. Rising from sleep, we cross into a new space. Doorways, gates, thresholds are all places of possibility, vibrant sacred markers of mystery. These thresholds in our lives are the markers of our leaving and becoming. We don't pay much attention to them, however. We recognize the threshold of our homes as the demarcation between public and private space, but our sense of this boundary has become rather fluid, and we allow unrestricted access to any number of outside interests to our personal sphere without debate or question, from work-related matters to social networking via the telephone, television or computer. Similarly, our grip on what is sacred and what is secular has become significantly eroded. We no longer understand how the former can use thresholds as transformational spaces where new possibilities arise and new visions are born.

Our casual treatment of thresholds is evident all around. We travel across continents and time zones at jet speed on our modern magic carpets, but lacking older wisdom, seldom allow our spirits time to catch up with our bodies. A young military chaplain friend of mine experienced this as a serious disconnect when he came back from Iraq to the United States. At first, he had trouble identifying what was keeping him feeling detached and split inside, but when we walked a short pilgrimage together to explore his reaction, he was able to recognize that he had crossed a demarcation point in his return without naming or marking it ritually and sacramentally. His physical body was home, but his spirit was still dislocated. He'd carried with him intense experiences and a hot anger that he had not fully acknowledged to himself. The secular, yellow ribbon homecoming celebrations were wonderful and important, but they focused more on his physical presence and safe return and failed to acknowledge that in many ways the man they welcomed back was not the same man who left. While he appreciated the ceremonies, they left him isolated and disconnected from others and also within himself, because they could not reach his heart's core. His complex feelings needed to be ritually recognized and honored, so that he could acknowledge, along with happiness and relief, his deep-seated memories that included profound grief and anger.

Many threshold spaces possess the creative capacity to transform us due to their form and design. For in these spaces, art and science come together, elevating our hearts and minds, and rooting us in the creative order. The labyrinth at Chartres is an extraordinary construction of both elegant, geometric precision and profound artistic expression. Human beings are more receptive to material forms and images than to ideas and intellectual constructs, since intellectual prowess is a skill that comes at a later developmental stage. That is why special, numinous spaces can speak to us directly, bypassing the logical, sequential part of our brains and connecting us with our deep selves and the cosmos.

When we look at a labyrinth for perhaps the first time, we are arrested by its design and begin to wonder about its strange circular configuration. It demands our attention. We register immediately in some place of our knowing that it represents ceremonial ground, a place of ritual and purpose, a consecrated space. At the same time, it both invites and attracts us while offering a warning against too casual a familiarity.

To enter a labyrinth is to cross a threshold. Our spirit knows this, even if our logical mind doesn't always comprehend it. The ancients well understood the power—and danger—of crossing a sacred threshold. They placed great stone lions, gargoyles, monsters and dragons at the entrances of their temples to symbolically alert our spirits it was time to wake up and pay attention. These fierce guardians were also meant to repel negative energy and discourage outsiders from entering. At the entrance of Ely Cathedral in Cambridgeshire, England, there is a small labyrinth that was installed in 19th century. Local folklore, as it was related to me, suggests that the purpose of this labyrinth was to confuse the devil. He would run into the labyrinth thinking it was the path into the cathedral where he could grab all the good souls engaged in worship, but the single path of the labyrinth would send him right back to where he came from, while the folks inside laughed at him! This was told to me with great good humor, but also illustrates how the threshold—in this case a labyrinth—functions as a place of demarcation and discrimination for engaging the sacred.

John O' Donohue in his book *To Bless the Space Between Us*, makes the point that thresholds should be considered as not merely transition points, but significant places of crossing and discernment. He reminds us that the root of the word comes from threshing: to separate the chaff from the grain. The process of traversing significant threshold space changes us. We do not return as entirely the same person.

Not only individuals, but whole cultures can cross thresholds to arrive at new ways of explaining the world and giving life meaning. When the 17th century French philosopher Renè Descartes proclaimed his famous *cogito ergo sum,* he ushered in an explosion of factual, scientific knowledge and discoveries. But while the results led to tremendous technological accomplishments (we could not imagine our present-day world without them), they also occurred, I believe, at the expense of other important ways of knowing our surroundings. The Age of Enlightenment separated us from mystery and a direct relationship with Mother Earth, and many of our feelings of alienation, isolation and aloneness can be attributed to that division.

Mircea Eliade, the religious historian, examining the foundations of belief systems, addressed this spiritual sickness and psychic split of the modern world. In *The Sacred and The Profane: The Nature of Religion*, he writes about the two modes of being in the world and the division of reality, which has us occupying the secular world as detached, fact-finding observers as a result of

> ...*the gigantic transformation of the world undertaken by the industrial societies, a transformation made possible by the desacralization of the cosmos accomplished by scientific thought and above all by the sensational discoveries of physics and chemistry.*

We, living in the 21st century, can't turn the clock back to a pre-Enlightenment culture. We have dropped the atom bomb, landed on the moon, invented computers, developed amazing treatments for disease and sickness, and produced scientific miracles beyond imagining, but we also experience existential isolation and separation by living mainly in Eliade's "profane" world.

What's the alternative? Goethe, the German poet, observing that beginnings have an energy and power to them, wrote, "Whatever you can do, or dream you can, begin it. Boldness has genius, power and magic in it." By crossing thresholds and entering "margin" countries, where the worlds of the sacred and profane intersect, we who dwell mostly in the world of the profane can touch the deep mysteries and realities not normally accessible to us. To walk a labyrinth is to cross such a threshold and go on a transformative journey. Even though this mini pilgrimage may be only brief physically, it may travel many leagues spiritually. In going on such a journey, we risk confronting our deepest fears and engaging in soul care, thus reconciling and resacralizing our lives. Is there a more important task for our age?

Chapter Six

Pilgrimage & Journey

Journeys bring power and love
Back into you. If you can't go somewhere,
Move into the passageways of the self.
They are like shafts of light,
Always changing, and you change
When you explore them.

—Rumi

The longest journey is the journey inwards.

—Dag Hammarskjold

From deep in our very bones, we are people of journey, a pilgrim race. A mournful train whistle cutting the silence of night, an open road, a pluming wake fanning out behind the speeding boat, the robotic voice of an airport loudspeaker system—all create a frisson of anticipation in our hearts. The voyage, the trip, the outing, the walk, all excite us, breaking open the pilgrim self and call our spirits to once again set forth. Brian Swimme, the cosmologist theologian, sees us as cosmic travelers in the emergent universe. We have come on a very long journey.

The journey in the labyrinth mirrors the journey of life and is archetypal. It is the birth, death and resurrection story. This makes it very powerful. We are walking a path that is in harmony with the natural order.

I received a wonderful example and model of this harmony as pilgrimage from the Rt. Rev. Marc Andrus, Episcopal Bishop of California, who is a true pilgrim soul himself. He points out that every pilgrimage—whether long or short—mirrors the great migratory journeys taken by creatures of the planet: fish, butterflies and birds. Many of them make amazing journeys to far off places where they mate and give birth to their offspring before returning to their place of origin. The great migrations of Monarch butterflies, hummingbirds, loons, geese and salmon are well documented and take place for the survival and future of their species. The creatures start in their normal habitat and go on a journey to a distant place where they hatch their eggs. But the journey does not stop there. To assure that the cycle life continues, they must then escort the new hatchlings back to the place of origin to begin the cycle anew.

David Quammen, who has studied these migrations, writes in the November 2010 issue of "National Geographic" of the intensity of purpose and special behaviors of these voyagers. They get ready for the ordeal by overfeeding and storing energy. Once they have begun a migration, they do not deviate, and will not respond to outside stimuli which would normally distract. They respond to a meta-purpose, to which all else is secondary.

These great migratory journeys are radical, dangerous acts, and the act of true pilgrimage symbolically bears the stamp of their three-fold nature. We begin at a particular place in our lives, in the mess of our everyday existence, and from there travel to a place of blessing where new opportunity, new ideas and new possibilities are born. But then we must bring those possibilities back to the place where we started. Our lives and future depend upon this circular pattern.

There is another life-giving, three-stage journey that exists inside our very bodies—our circulatory system. Oxygen-depleted blood cells first trickle, then flow from our extremities through the venous pathways to the center, the heart and lungs, where they receive the life-sustaining gift of oxygen from the outside. Re-oxygenated, the blood cells are pumped back through the arterial channels, carrying the gift of life into every part of the body.

This three-fold pattern of circulating blood and the great journeys of animal migration mirrors the path of every pilgrimage. It starts in one place in our lives and takes us towards a goal, which may be physically close by or far away. Regardless, the psychic, spiritual distance traveled is often immense. The center, or goal, is a place of blessing and illumination, whose gift is for the entire community, not just for our individual selves. Of course, blessings may accrue anywhere along the way. The path back home is a time for integration, so that the pilgrim who arrives home can share the blessings with the world.

To walk the labyrinth is to go on a pilgrimage—the journey of a three-fold path—albeit a short one. It is a both an exterior and interior journey, and though people express multiple reasons for taking it, at the heart is the need for reconnection and reconciliation (putting things right again). At the deepest level, though almost never consciously expressed, it is about the resacralization of the world. People sense that "the time is out of joint," and this feeling of dis-ease urges us to get off our couches and embark on a journey. The grail quest of our time is nothing less than reconciliation of the worlds of the profane and the sacred which we have lost, engendering a meaningful future and offering hope for a warring world. This is the work of heroes and soul warriors!

A vivid example of this need to relieve the pain of the world, to walk for healing, wholeness, and connection in the numbness of disaster is reported by David Willis McCullough in his book *The Unending Mystery: A Journey Through Labyrinths and Mazes*. After the catastrophe of 9/11, as the smoke still rose over the ruins of the twin towers of the World Trade Center, people cleared off the layers of ash and debris at Trinity Church on Wall Street and made a labyrinth, which they then walked during their lunch hours as a prayer for peace and for those in pain. In Lower Manhattan's Battery Park, they constructed another labyrinth for healing. All across the country, people walked labyrinths at that terrible time.

Similarly, after the devastation of Hurricane Katrina, people walked the labyrinth in several places along the shores of Gulf Coast. Since then, several beautiful labyrinths have been constructed in New Orleans. One was built in Audubon Park by Marty Kermeen as a symbol of hope and new beginning. Following the tragic oil spill in the Gulf of Mexico in the summer of 2010, people walked labyrinths on the beaches, wherever they made or found them. They walked as the oil washed up, clogging marshes and coating seabirds and wild life. When the catastrophic tsunami rolled across the Japanese coastlands in 2011, leaving devastation in its wake and raising the specter of nuclear disaster, people across the world began walking!

Having experienced the terrible intensity of disaster, we seek a balancing intensity in our spiritual life that can provide some meaning, so that we don't remain trapped in a never-ending downward spiral of chaos. This need for what will address our depth of emotion and feeling cannot be satisfied by talking and intellectual activity—it requires a body-based form: Walking a labyrinth, going on pilgrimage, visiting and circumambulating sacred wells of healing can all fill that need. Cloisters were constructed in churches, temples and monasteries not because of some architect's whimsical fancy, but because people from different religious traditions across the globe have found that the act of walking in a circular fashion while meditating and praying allows for the synthesis of ideas and creativity. As we move in the rhythm of the circle, the kinetic energy of the body is released, stilling the tyranny of the controlling mind and allowing our creative juices to begin to flow.

The human need to go on pilgrimages to visit sacred places wells up from within. It cannot be controlled by any institution, nor its officials, although they often wish to appropriate the released energy and claim its vitality. Most religions use the ceremony and ritual associated with journey because they are so powerful, but while professional religious practitioners or secular officials may try to control the experience, ultimately, it is the people who decide how to walk and pray and what needs to be done to access the sacred.

A friend of mine, the Reverend Dale Clem, who used to live in Lithuania, told me the story of an extraordinary pilgrimage site there: The Hill of Crosses. The history of that small Baltic country, sandwiched between Prussia and the Russian Empire, was one of a series of occupations by invading forces. Several centuries ago, a village was razed, and in remembrance, people began to bring crosses to the site. They continued that pilgrimage practice over the opposition of the many different authorities in power. In time, the hill, which is only 100 feet high and covered with crosses, has become a place of national prayer and pilgrimage for freedom. The crosses are sometimes adorned with pictures of the Virgin or images of those who were deported or killed during the Nazi and Soviet invasions. There are crosses planted in grief, in giving thanks, in hope and in despair. It is an amazing potpourri of folk art, kitsch and sacred intention, yet indisputably powerful. During the years of Soviet occupation, the Communists frequently bulldozed the hill and its crosses. But by night, pilgrims kept coming with equal determination, and the crosses with their adornment of pictures and written prayers kept rising on the hill's slopes. Finally in 1985, Gorbachev conceded and said, "Let them have their hill." In 1990, Lithuania announced its independence. Today the hill blossoms with crosses and images.

In the same way that Lithuanians insisted that the Hill of Crosses remain a deeply sacred place and destination, people of today have decided that the labyrinth is an important sacred pilgrimage site for our time, after centuries of neglect since the Age of Reason.

As I have argued before, labyrinth walks are mini-pilgrimages, so it is worth looking at the major reasons why people undertake these sacred journeys. And we will come to see some of these reasons reflected in those who walk the way of the prayer path of the labyrinth.

Justice

Pilgrimage often has a call for justice at its heart. Deep in our spirits, we crave a just society where there is no tyranny and everyone is honored equally. When justice is denied, the soul rises up, sometimes leading to great pilgrimages to obtain redress of grievances. The classic example is the biblical account of Exodus, in which the Hebrews sought to escape the yoke of Egyptian bondage, but there are many others. Gandhi's great salt march to the sea was a pilgrimage for freedom and justice. So were the great Civil Rights marches in the American South.

Obligation

One journey of duty that comes to mind is the great Haj pilgrimage that Muslim faithful should take at least once during a lifetime. We recognize the same cry of obligation echoing down the centuries in "Next year in Jerusalem," as Jews acknowledge the call of place and history, hoping at least once to visit the Holy City. In Christianity, the Stations of the Cross are the pilgrimage that is taken every Holy Week as people ritually enact the sacred circle of birth, life, suffering and death of Jesus followed by the resurrection and new life.

Healing

Restoration of health and healing has been a major focus of pilgrimage from time immemorial. Sacred wells and circles are often known as healing places. The labyrinth fits very well into this therapeutic category. As modern hospitals recognize the importance of spiritual health as well as physical well-being, they have begun in increasing numbers to incorporate labyrinths into their wellness offerings for patients and their families.

Restoration and Integration

In brokenness, we desire the healing balm of reconciliation. The Umbau School of Architecture in Virginia wanted to construct a labyrinth in Sarajevo as a way of offering a meaningful, interdenominational, physical path to wholeness for the inhabitants of a city that had been ripped apart by religious and ethnic warfare after the breakup of Yugoslavia.

Forgiveness

Confession is one of the soul's deepest needs, so naming and claiming past misdeeds is the focus of many journeys. By acknowledging and connecting with our history, we can begin to lay old ghosts to rest. Many people use the labyrinth as a place to ritually express contrition for what they have done and to claim forgiveness and sacred acceptance of their lives. Today, labyrinths have their place in many prisons. In San Francisco, the Rev. Davidson Bidwell-Waite uses a labyrinth to help gang members begin to find their own authentic life path, instead of following the destructive ruts of gang membership.

Finding a heart for forgiveness is always a challenge, no matter what the circumstances, but for families who have experienced the violence of murder, it is extraordinarily difficult. The wounds are continually being reopened by parole board hearings, publicity and a history that never seems to resolve. In circumstances like these, the grace of the labyrinth and deep prayer are helpful. People sometimes put down pictures of a murdered family member along the way. Or they ask everyone who walks with them to pray for strength and courage in parole board hearings. Sometimes they ask that they can open their heart to find forgiveness, too.

Seasons and anniversaries

People may be stirred by the season, because it's the summer solstice, or by as simple a reason as that winter is over. Labyrinth walks in preparation for life-changing events, such as chemotherapy treatments, retirement, impending death or birth are common ways of addressing these physical and spiritual transitions. In India, the time when children are grown and the financial responsibilities of protecting the family are taken care of is recognized as an important period in people's lives, and they may go on a pilgrimage to mark the transition to new demands which focus on the spirit, not only the day-to-day struggles of business and family.

As I have noted several times already, the hunger for pilgrimage also has to do with our hunger for the Holy. We all need to heal the schizoid rift between sacred and profane worlds. Far too few churches and religious institutions today are nourishing the soul hunger of our time, so people are taking the matter into their own hands and setting forth on their own. As a multi-faceted experience, pilgrimage is both physical and spiritual, thus eliminating the great Cartesian split of mind over matter.

Heeding the call of our deeper selves, crossing thresholds, and juggling the ambiguities of multiple realities require an open heart and soul, and a willingness to learn and stretch both physical and spiritual muscles. It takes practice and a sense of humor, as well. Lao Tzu observed, "The longest journey starts with a single step." So start small, and embrace the risk to transform throughout the journey.

Chapter Seven

The Way of a Warrior

They shall grow not old, as we that are left grow old:
Age shall not weary them, nor the years contemn.
At the going down of the sun and in the morning
We will remember them.

—Laurence Binyon

The Hallmark Company has made millions of dollars by recognizing the importance of special days in our national consciousness and providing cards for most of our civic, secular holidays, anniversaries and celebrations. But these public expressions are often charged with extremely complex emotions, and the civic secular acknowledgments can only touch a small part of the depth of feeling lying below the surface.

One such occasion is Veteran's Day, a national holiday created after World War I to honor the soldiers who served their country by fighting in the carnage of Europe at the beginning of the 20th century. The significance of the holiday has expanded to cover all veterans and their families, and those who serve and support them. There are parades, speeches, the laying of wreaths and the playing of taps. All of these rituals are important recognitions of our obligation to the members of our armed forces, past and present. However, they do not generally allow for private expressions of anxiety, prayer and grief. These ceremonies do not usually facilitate a sacred meeting of the individual's story with the Holy through ritual. A human being's experience moves from the particular to the universal. It is much more difficult to do the reverse and shift down from the collective, big picture to the smaller story of our own individual lives. This is where a labyrinth walk can be a powerful ritual of connection.

While I was director of a center for pilgrimage and reconciliation at the Church of the Nativity in Huntsville, Alabama, we decided to hold a special Veteran's Day labyrinth event. We wanted this to be an intergenerational experience honoring our armed forces and allowing veterans to tell a new generation what the day meant to them. Accordingly, we placed advertisements in the local newspaper and the Redstone Arsenal's gazette about our program and intentions. We invited a high school JROTC cadet group and their leader to lunch with veterans of World War II. The young people ate with the veterans, and it was a good time of sharing stories and experiences. Following the lunch, the students all made an honor walk of the labyrinth for the members of our armed forces who were currently serving around the world. Many of the students had friends and family members in the military, and they appreciated the opportunity to ritually honor their service and commitment.

A chill rain dampened that dark, cold November afternoon, and after the students left, I thought about closing the labyrinth and going home. That's when he arrived, an old man bent over and walking in some pain, shuffling and dragging his feet. I'd never seen him before. He'd come in response to one of our advertisements. He asked for a few directions on how to walk a labyrinth and started out. As his feet followed the circular path, his body began to shake – it became obviously difficult for him to continue. I went to him to help him and said, "This is very hard for you, isn't it?" He nodded by way of acknowledgement then opened his hand. In his palm he held a crumpled, tear-stained piece of paper with the names of all his World War II comrades. "All dead," he murmured, "all dead." Together we lit a candle for each of his friends and placed their names on a prayer list. Afterwards, he said, "I didn't understand why I had to come here this afternoon. Thank you, now I know."

I never saw the old man again, but I have often thought about him and his story. I thought about how he held all his friends in his heart over the long years, perhaps wondering why he was alive and they were not. A labyrinth is a place of connection, a place where the boundaries between realities are permeable: The living and the dead are close. In this walk, the old man was not alone; he walked with the "great cloud of witnesses" (Hebrews 12:1) and in the communion of the saints. He must have attended countless Veteran's Day parades and ceremonies in his long life, yet it took the quiet intimacy, the heart space and prayer on the labyrinth for his tears to flow allowing him to lay down his grief.

Over several years of offering the labyrinth on Veteran's Day, I encountered many different people. I saw mothers who walked praying for their children serving in the armed forces. I witnessed anguished mothers who walked in grief for their children who had died in battle. I observed old soldiers walking as though on parade, backs straight, on guard, honoring the memories of their fallen comrades. I saw the reconciling power that a walk on the labyrinth can unleash and realized that the civic ceremonies did not reach deep enough into the soul space of wounded people. But that is not really their purpose anyway. In order to be politically correct, our civic ceremonies have been watered down in order not to offend anyone's sensibilities. In actuality, however, no watering down is needed. What is required is the willingness to go deeper into understanding the history of ancient ways and wisdom. The powerful, substantive meaning in the subterranean aquifer running through the foundations of our history and bedrock of our culture and being can still be tapped for its healing balm, but only by those who are willing to go beneath and beyond the surface of civic ceremony.

As we welcome home veterans from overseas wars in Iraq and Afghanistan, it is of vital importance that we give them and their families a sacred space in which to integrate their experiences. Bethesda Naval Hospital is beginning labyrinth work. But that is just one facility, and our veterans and their families are spread across the country. Training skilled labyrinth facilitators and companions becomes the next critical step to help them all begin to turn the page and begin a new chapter of their life.

Chapter Eight

The Power of Ritual

To turn, turn will be our delight
Till by turning, turning,
we come down right.

—Shaker hymn

When we go on pilgrimage or walk a labyrinth, we engage in a complex ritual act that impacts us on physical, emotional and even historical levels. Ritual changes lives in profound ways, but it has gotten a bad rap in today's secular world. Cynics sarcastically dismiss religious practice as "just empty ritual." Indeed, "empty" and "meaningless" are the two adjectives I frequently hear associated with the word "ritual" by those who have no understanding of the profound nature of its discipline and practice.

I remember a devout woman who was married to a physician who never attended church. When I asked her about this, she told me that he couldn't deal with the "mumbo jumbo" of ritual—he was a scientist. How ironic, since he engaged in ritual every day in his work life. In the secular world, almost no place is more fraught with ritual than a hospital. It is very much like a temple where the doctors, high priests robed in scrubs and masks, preside at the inner sanctum of the operating room, divine illnesses by studying mysterious black-and-white images of the insides of our bodies on flickering light boxes, and scribble their healing "spells" illegibly on pieces of paper prescribing pills and potions.

Many people also reject ritual as too conservative and repetitious in our multi-media, high-speed entertainment and communication-driven age. But when these same people are introduced to ritual in the context of their own life story and the seemingly dead symbolic synapses fire up, their consciousness reawakens and they have a transformative experience no digital electronic medium can provide. So we are back to the importance of story and narrative in the design of ritual.

Joseph Campbell, the mythologist and writer on comparative religion, observed that people usually cannot move from one life state of being to another without ritual. The sexually abused children I described earlier needed a ritual to help them change their stories and let go of a destructive part of their lives. Ritual can benefit people seeking forgiveness for themselves or others, or trying to find a new life after divorce. It can provide soldiers returning from war with a context for integration of their story. The ritual of labyrinth walks, in which people can put down the heavy weights they've carried, ceremonially burn letters, or place pictures of remembrance, facilitates healing and grace. There is no end to the rituals we can imagine to help us on the road to freedom and new life. For labyrinth trainers and companions, this is a rich area for further development.

In the North American culture, where "talk therapy" is frequently the preferred medium for personal transformation, we have forgotten that experience must precede reflection and that we "think" with our bodies. As ritual allows the physical body to enact the new state of being or consciousness, it opens the door to new possibilities and realities. While it has the power to change us, ritual also provides structure to our lives. Initiation ceremonies throughout the world not only transport aspirants to different levels of engagement within a community, they also define groups and reinforce their cohesion by revealing who is "in" and who is "out."

One way to look at the power of ritual is to see it as a scaffold providing structure for life. From when we get up in the morning to our going to bed at night, we follow many rituals. We walk the dog down a certain path, drive the same way to work, approach our day at the office by following established patterns, and so on. Ritual action and behavior tells us who we are and, just as importantly, who we are not. People with bad table manners are out of place at an elegant dinner party. People who are rigid and fastidious will feel deeply uncomfortable on a wilderness camping trip.

Children love ritual, and parents that either boldly or carelessly decide to change the ritual surrounding family ceremonies and feasts do so at their peril. Unknowingly, I tried altering the menu one Christmas Eve and was loudly criticized by my children and husband who felt cheated of an important part of their remembered experience. At Thanksgiving, it is customary for a host to ask guests what foods are part of their Thanksgiving tradition, and to make sure they are part of the meal.

The only ritual we still concede some genuine force to transform us is the marriage ceremony. However much we might want to disown its sacred power, we acknowledge that two separate people become one, and that their lives are transformed.

Whether we like it or not, there's no way to avoid rituals. In *To Heal a Fractured World: The Ethics of Responsibility*, Rabbi Jonathan Sacks has this to say about the importance of the role of ritual:

> Far too little attention has been paid to the role of ritual in the moral life.... All I can say is that ritual is to ethics what physical exercise is to health. Medical knowledge alone will not make me healthy. That requires daily discipline, a ritual—and religion is the matrix of ritual.

When our modern age rejects ritual associated with the sacred, it does so without understanding its intrinsic healing power or its profound influence on our ethical, moral life. For the old soldier who came to walk the labyrinth, past, present and future were conflated into Now. In the sacred center of the labyrinth, he could reconnect with his long dead comrades in arms. In the context of his story, they reached across time and were mystically present.

In *Natural Grace: Dialogues on Creation, Darkness, and the Soul in Spirituality and Science*, Matthew Fox and Rupert Sheldrake write about this unusual time-space continuum property of ritual:

> The purpose of ritual is to connect the present participants with the original event that the ritual commemorates and also to link them with all those who have participated in the ritual in the past. Ritual is something to do with crossing time, annihilating distance in time, bringing the past into the present.

Eliade also refers to this curious property of ritual to conflate time when he writes about *in illud tempore*—ritual suspending time for its participants, allowing them to experience past and present as one.

At the same time, we exist physically and matter matters. We inhabit our body suits, yet they do not represent the totality of our being. Teilhard de Chardin comments that we are spiritual beings on a human journey and gives credence to both: What happens to the spirit affects the body, and what happens to the body affects the spirit. That is why physical prayer and ritual are so important. Pilgrimage, journey, labyrinth walks are concrete and dynamic processes for developing sacred imagination and engaging the non-rational part of our psyche.

The word "psyche" is rich in meaning, referring not only to the human soul or spirit, but also to the mental or psychological structure of a person, especially as it operates as a motive force. The psyche appreciates mystery, relationship and connectedness, but it cannot distinguish between ritual and event. Nor can it differentiate between people or situations, so events, persons and time can be conflated, and one person or location may substitute for another. At night, our psyche offers vivid symbolic interpretations of the dilemmas we face, for dreams are the psyche's natural territory. In our sleep, we examine our internal and external questions, dreaming symbolic possibilities which the conscious, logical mind has rejected.

The body-based language of ceremony and ritual that feeds the spirit is associated with non-directed, primary thinking; it is intuitive, with no separation between assumption and fact. It is also the language of the labyrinth, where paradox and contradictions can co-exist (the bush in Exodus 3 burns, but does not burn); past, present and future hold hands; the world of dreams and creativity is rich; and language is expressive and affective instead of intellectual and rational. It is a way of thinking and being that we disregard at our peril, because what is not acknowledged goes into deep unconscious. But while it is no longer accessible to us, it will not be denied its power and existence. Its energy will flare up in distorted ways and strange places.

Our daily news is filled with instances of projection and substitution, where a victim of an assault may have had no prior contact with the attacker, but becomes a "stand-in" for another person or event. The killers at Columbine High in their murderous rampage were slaughtering "representatives" of those they wanted to destroy. Their psyches had substituted anyone in their cross hairs for people they believed had originally hurt them.

Robert Johnson has this to say about the power of ritual and ceremony to subvert these distortions in his book, *Owning Your Own Shadow: Understanding the Dark Side of the Psyche*:

> *All healthy societies have a rich ceremonial life. Less healthy ones rely on unconscious expressions: War, violence, psychosomatic illness, neurotic suffering, and accidents are very low-grade ways of living out the shadow. Ceremony and ritual are a far more intelligent means of accomplishing the same thing.*

The paradoxical-thinking attribute of the psyche is most present in the minds of artists, musicians, dramatists and story tellers, but as we age and gain some maturity, some of us can engage it as well by letting go of polarized thinking which demands only right or wrong, black or white answers. As we begin to embrace the "both/and" possibility of paradox, we come closer to the place where sacred truth dwells. Perhaps that is one of the reasons why Jesus welcomed children so wholeheartedly and encouraged us all to have the spirit of the child. A child's imagination has no difficulty holding tensions and opposites, as anyone who has told stories to children can affirm: The prince is a frog or a bear; the princess is the woodcutter's daughter; toys come to life and a nutcracker is a soldier defeating the hordes of the Mouse King; shape-shifting is an everyday occurrence; animals speak and multiple transformative possibilities coexist. At the same time as they accept these contradictory images, children are not delusional. They are also in touch with the more mundane reality in which we live most of our lives. Speaking of the growing child, the poet William Wordsworth wonderfully describes this "magical" or primary-based thinking in his "Ode on the Intimations of Immortality":

> *But he beholds the light, and whence it flows,*
> *He sees it in his joy;*
> *The Youth, who daily farther from the east*
> *Must travel, still is Nature's priest,*
> *And by the vision splendid*
> *Is on his way attended;*
> *At length the Man perceives it die away,*
> *And fade into the light of common day.*

The plasticity of the psyche can be used powerfully in ritual on a labyrinth walk or other type of pilgrimage to defuse and deflect psychic toxicity.

A few years ago in the Castro district of San Francisco, The Rev. Diana Wheeler put a canvas labyrinth down on the pavement at an outdoor worship event and invited people to walk. Shortly afterwards, when a young man was killed in the area, she was asked by several people in the community to bring the labyrinth back for a time of healing. The people recognized the need for ritual and sacred space in which to place and reconcile their grief and anger at the violence of the murder. They needed a space that was accessible to everyone whatever their faith background, and the labyrinth answered their needs.

An example of how a repressed experience can suddenly erupt into the present comes from a workshop I held on forgiveness. As we were doing an exercise that involved the use of rubber gloves, Elaine, one of the participants, suddenly became distressed, flushed and angry. Sobbing, she explained that years ago her brother, with whom she had been very close, had contracted AIDS. It was at the beginning of the outbreak when people didn't know much about the disease, and everyone was very scared. Her brother had been hospitalized in total isolation. His family and the hospital staff were not allowed to touch him—everyone had to wear gowns, masks and rubber gloves. Tragically, her brother died without the grace of any human, caring touch. Elaine knew in her head that she was not to blame for this, but after all these years, she still carried a weight of guilt, grief and anger in her heart. The exercise with the gloves triggered the hidden rage, and her unconscious erupted in tears and fury. When she wondered how to let go of the pain and anger she still felt because of hospital's isolation procedures, we talked about it and she decided take an armful of rubber gloves into the labyrinth and hurl them one after the other into the center. As she performed this ritual, venting her rage and fury at the institution and her grief over her brother's death, she gave them to the center of the labyrinth, a sacred container that was big enough to hold them.

Chapter Nine

The Spirit/Body Connection

You, sent out beyond your recall,
go to the limits of your longing.
Embody me.
Flare up like flame
and make big shadows I can move in.
Let everything happen to you: beauty and terror.
Just keep going. No feeling is final.
Don't let yourself lose me.
Nearby is the country they call life.
You will know it by its seriousness.
Give me your hand.

—Rainer Maria Rilke

We western societies know abstractly that the world of the body and the world of the psyche and spirit are interconnected. Nothing can happen to one without creating an impact on the other. We seldom pay much attention to this relation, however, until our bodies make us face our spiritual pain by becoming sick. We have a heart attack, get cirrhosis of the liver, develop diabetes, or suffer any of the other sicknesses that may reflect a life that's lived in a fractured fashion.

How a labyrinth helps restore the balance between body and spirit is a very modern question, and in some ways not a helpful one, since there is a dimension of the experience that lies in the realm of the mystical, beyond the probing of neuroscience and psychology. It's also a question that demonstrates a need for control. My son, who has a very stressful job, claims that walking the labyrinth when he's experiencing high anxiety calms him and resets his equilibrium. I think this is an interesting observation. Children who have ADD find that after using the labyrinth, they can settle down and concentrate for longer periods of time. A friend of mine in San Francisco works with street people. One of her contacts is a woman who has lived a life of what most of us would consider unspeakable horror. When they meet, my friend brings a large box of crayons and many pages of labyrinth outlines. They sit and have coffee while the street lady colors the labyrinths. At first her coloring is wild and disorganized, but after a while calms down and becomes less frenetic. As the woman herself becomes more relaxed, they begin to talk.

I have heard an explanation that the quadrants of the labyrinth mirror the quadrants in the brain, and that crossing them on the way to the center, or the hippocampus of the brain, evens out the energy flow causing a sense of renewed balance and a greater ability to concentrate. Is this true? I don't know, but for whatever reason, walking the labyrinth does have physiological effects that involve reduction of anxiety and frenetic activity, while at the same time generating more focused energy.

Sometimes people use finger labyrinths that are mirror images of each other and trace the paths in order to achieve emotional balance. Trying to draw labyrinths as mirror images, using the left and right hand simultaneously is yet another way to restore spiritual/emotional balance. This requires quite a bit of practice, as the dominant hand and corresponding side of the brain try to take over without allowing the other to catch up, but it's an exercise that is very revealing and worth attempting.

The labyrinth has a way sometimes of focusing the spirit/body connection and helping us to see what it is we're dealing with. The following stories show how this connection was made for two people I met.

A consortium of clinics in Mississippi wanted to hold a wellness fair and invited me to present the labyrinth as a tool for healing. As my team and I were setting up the labyrinth, I noticed a woman who kept poking her head round the door and looking at us. I didn't think much about it, figuring that she was one of the many people who were making sure the presenters in the fair had all the supplies they needed. Later, one of the organizers told me that this woman had vigorously opposed our participation because she believed that labyrinths represented magic and superstition, but she had been overruled. He told me this so that if she approached me, I'd be prepared. The fair opened and people began to walk the labyrinth.

At some point, the woman came through the door. She came hesitantly, looking at others walking. She absorbed the atmosphere of calm and movement. Then she came to me and said, "I don't know how to do this, but could I walk the labyrinth, too?" I gave her a few basic instructions and she took off her shoes and began to walk. Soon she was beginning to have trouble. She started limping and seemed to be in considerable pain. I wondered whether she would continue her walk, but she persevered. It was a large

labyrinth and it probably took her about 40 minutes
to get to the center and back out again. Throughout
the walk, she clearly had problems with her left foot,
although she had shown no evidence of pain when she
first entered the room.

When she finished her walk, she came towards me
and a young woman who was on our team. I asked her,
"What happened in the labyrinth? You seemed to be in
pain." She answered, "It was so strange, as soon as
I started walking, my foot cramped up, but I felt I needed
to continue." Louisa, my young friend, asked, "What
spiritual pain did you carry into the labyrinth with you?"
The woman looked at us with astonishment, and said,
"Oh! My son has just had his foot amputated, and
he's having a very hard time accepting this limitation.
The family is very upset about it." Then she realized
what she'd said, and that her body was expressing the
pain she carried in her heart and spirit around her son's
surgery. She was deeply moved and left quietly.

In the labyrinth, her body made explicit the anxiety that
she and her family were carrying about her son and physically
expressed her emotional pain. Clearly, this was not what
she had anticipated when she voiced her fear of magic and
superstition that she had associated with labyrinths. She
did not find magic—she found simply the truth about a life
situation she was confronting.

Another example of how the physical aspects of labyrinths
and pilgrimage can help us identify what we have been hiding
from ourselves happened during a labyrinth workshop in
California, where I met a man who was wrestling with inner
demons that were only partly conscious for him.

During the workshop I spent time talking about the different aspects of the labyrinth walk, indentifying the three different stages: Releasing, Receiving, and the path back, Integration. One of the participants, a young man named Jason, paid intense attention. I stayed in touch with him after the session, and he told me at some point that he had frequently walked the labyrinth in Grace Cathedral, San Francisco, on his own, but that he consistently lost his way on the path out from the center: The path of Integration. Somehow, he always ended up on the wrong path and became confused. Jason was a very orderly man and struggling with owning his sexual identity. Although married, he was gay and deeply closeted even to himself. But while confused, he was also curious about his seeming inability to follow a simple instruction: Stay on the path. He knew that in some way it was significant for him and pointed to a place in his life that needed attention and exploration. For Jason, this recurring misstep on the path of Integration provided the impetus to look further and deeper at what he was refusing to integrate himself. It took him a little while, but since he was a man of courage, he eventually claimed his true identity, the part he had kept hidden.

A variation of Jason's story is frequently part of the labyrinth path for members of the GLBT (Gay, Lesbian, Bi-sexual, Transgendered) community as they seek to discern who they are.

Pilgrimage in any form often jogs the unconscious into awareness of unresolved issues. As a companion guide, I have travelled with other pilgrims who, like Jason, were wrestling with their sexual identity, only to have pieces of the puzzle come together during or shortly after the journey. Anyone who makes a serious voyage of self-discovery will run onto shoals or hidden reefs. These obstacles are actually markers that point the way toward self-knowledge and acceptance. Sexual identity is just one reef. There are plenty of others.

Chapter Ten

Stories and "Aha" Moments

*The destiny of the world is determined less
by the battles that are lost and won
than by the stories it loves and believes in.*

—Harold Goddard

Most of the time when people walk a labyrinth, it is just a simple walk. Lightening doesn't strike with bolts of recognition, no epiphanies occur. We may return to our daily lives gently calmed, refreshed and energized. There are occasions, however, when we are walking with a special intention that it's as if a breath of fresh air blows away the mists and cobwebs of our psyche and we experience a particular clarity and grace.

Sometimes, life tosses us challenges that demand spiritual resources we have never bothered to cultivate and don't think we possess. When this happens, we feel vulnerable, alone and bereft. At that point, a physical act, such as walking a labyrinth or going on pilgrimage, can bring reassurance, allow us to face our fears, reveal our true identity to us, and even open up new directions or dimensions in our lives.

The following stories illustrate a variety of responses to the labyrinth.

Monica was a well-to-do middle-aged woman who was always immaculately dressed. She lived in a spacious, elegant house in the best part of town in a Midwestern city and was not in obvious want of anything. But when her third husband, who had taken good care of her, unexpectedly died, her spirits plummeted and she grieved deeply for him and for herself. During this period of mourning, she also became critically ill and found out that she needed to have radical heart surgery. She was terrified. How could she face this surgery on her own without the support and strength of her husband? It wasn't a lack of confidence in her doctors or the hospital staff – among the best in the country –it was the powerful sense of being completely alone for the first time in many years and having to undergo this life-or-death ordeal by herself without a man beside her. She had children, but they did not fill the hole in her heart and her life. How was she to claim her own courage and identity, the strength of being a full woman and human being, when she needed it most? That's a lot to demand of someone who seldom paid attention to these matters and spent her life under someone else's shadow and protection. She realized that the money that had bought her security and social acceptance wasn't valid tender in the shadowy counting house of sickness and death.

It was at this point that I met Monica. She was looking for spiritual strength and courage to go through her upcoming ordeal. I suggested a labyrinth walk and explained what would be involved and why she might want to do this. She agreed, but asked if she could bring something with her that belonged to her late husband, because she still could not imagine doing anything without him. She chose an old T-shirt that faintly smelled of him and clutched it close to her face as she entered the labyrinth. Then something happened. As Monica went deeper inside, slowly, without her noticing, she started to relax her grip. She carried the T-shirt gently in her hands, and as she reached the center, placed it on the ground. She emerged from the labyrinth with a rather bewildered look on her face, and said, "I left it in the middle." Then the awareness of what she'd done hit her. She realized that, along with the T-shirt, she'd left her dependency in the middle of the labyrinth and claimed her own life, identity, courage and strength! She said to me, "Oh, I see, I can do this by myself now." And she did.

Monica's story is powerful for many reasons. It demonstrates so strongly the body/spirit connection. Monica needed to ritually lay down her grief and dependency in a physical manner in order to recover her independence and accept a new identity. By walking the three-fold path of the labyrinth, she was able to let go of her fear and receive the gift of courage, gaining the confidence that she could deal with whatever lay ahead on her own. That's a lot to achieve in one short walk, yet Monica accomplished just that, and happily, the surgery was successful.

Here's another, quite different story that involves confronting spiritual and physical pain and imagining one's own ritual for new life.

Jane, a vivacious, highly intelligent woman, who ran a summer camp for "at risk" youth in Montana, asked me for help to introduce the labyrinth to a group of counselors. There was a large labyrinth on the grounds of a nearby church camp, and she had been wondering how to use it as part of the treatment for the young campers. A friend and I designed a day of instruction for the counselors, so that they could understand the labyrinth's power and incorporate it into their work

Although the surroundings were beautiful, with a bubbling stream nearby and hills in the background, the labyrinth itself was harsh. Its path consisted of a hard, heavy material coated with silica, not soft or welcoming like grass. To make matters worse, the afternoon of the training session the sun was blazing down and the heat had turned the silica on the path to burning glass. We suggested that the counselors keep their shoes on. All of them did, except Jane, who chose to remain barefoot. As she walked the labyrinth, she became visibly distressed. She had gone about three-quarters of the way when she couldn't stand the heat any longer and had to come out for her shoes. After she went back in the labyrinth, she spent a while in the center. Then she walked straight out of the labyrinth from the center, ignoring the path back, and stood off to one side withdrawn in silence.

Much later, Jane told me what happened to her on the walk. Several years before at another camp, one of the young girls participated in a wilderness hike in the mountains as part of the curriculum/treatment. Jane was a member of the counselor team, although she did not go on that particular hike herself. The day was very hot, and before long, one of the girls complained she wanted water, complained she wanted to stop, and complained she'd had enough and wanted to go home. But the lead counselor didn't listen to her, because the girl had a history of whining. Then, towards the end of the long, hot day, the young girl could go no further and fainted. The counselor looked at her lying on the trail and realized in horror that she was dying of heat exposure and dehydration. It was too late to save her.

The owners of the camp refused to discuss the death and its implications. Because they kept silent about the event, and did not address the deficiencies in staff training and lack of proper emergency prepared-ness, no one was able to move forward. Although she was not directly involved or responsible, Jane carried the burden of this death in her heart for years. The fact that she had not known how to change the system and perhaps didn't have the ability at the time to con-front the wall of implacable, corporate silence did not matter. She told me that she had gone into the laby-rinth barefooted because she wanted to experience the pain of unbearable heat, so she would gain forgiveness and release from the soul weight she carried due to her unwilling collusion in the conspiracy of silence. Al-though it didn't look like it at the time, she did find fire, release and blessing in the labyrinth that day.

Jane's story is a wonderful example of someone who imagined her own ritual for healing No longer willing to live a life that was divided, she used the opportunity to let go of her history and claim her own truth.

Another story of soul healing comes from a lovely black woman from South Africa, Kagiso. She had come with a group on a mission trip to the United States to talk with members of different churches about the work they were doing with the Truth and Reconciliation Commission and how it created the foundation for a better future for her country. It was a powerful presentation of resolution and overturning a system of lies and domination. However, Kagiso had her own personal pain, and when a friend and I met with Kagiso at a day of relaxation for the South African delegation, we realized how much personal pain she carried. As we lounged in deck chairs by a swimming pool, sipping cokes and chatting, she told us her story.

Kagiso came from a privileged background, so certain members of her family had dealings with the white apartheid government. These contacts with the "oppressor state" became the object of suspicion among some factions and gangs in the black townships. For one of her relatives, it resulted in death by necklacing, the barbaric practice of putting an old tire over the victim's head, filling with gasoline and setting it on fire. The gang responsible for this horrific execution took Kagiso and the rest of her family and made them watch what would happen to a "snitch." The terrible scene was branded into her mind's eye forever. Later on, she herself became a victim of rape.

After we listened to her appalling tale, we explored with her whether she would like to walk the labyrinth as a way of ritually letting go of the past and its legacy of bondage and death. Kagiso agreed. She, like the sexually abused children from the NCAC, decided to carry a heavy rock during her journey. She told us later that as she walked, the rock became the weight of the world in her hands; it was literally unbearable. But she still hung on, determined to carry the familiar burden until finally she decided to let go of the pain.

Kagiso did not put the rock down gently, she let it go and it fell with a thundering crash to the floor, sending reverberations of finality in all directions. She told us afterward that she now realized why she'd had to make the trip to the United States—it wasn't only for the mission work she'd been doing with the group, it was to walk the labyrinth to get rid of the stones in her heart, allowing images of a death by fire to be transformed into the fire of compassion for her country, her family and herself.

What is so striking about people who have allowed a sacred ritual to help them cross a new threshold is that they feel themselves to be a different person, literally. The past is past for them; it no longer has a grip on them. Of course, it will always be a part of their history and experience, but it is just a chapter now, not the whole book. When people can get to the point of owning their suffering and letting it go, they become a powerful force for the blessing of others on the road. They are truly touched by the Fire of Pentecost, a fire that burns but does not destroy, a fire that brings forth new life from the ashes.

Because some labyrinth journey stories are so powerful, many people are concerned when they don't experience similar lightning bolts of revelation. They think that the walk didn't work. This is to misunderstand the nature of the labyrinth and its gentle, subtle ways. For most walks and pilgrimages, just the act of embarking on a journey resets our direction. Sometimes the intention of setting out and just being on the path is enough. It doesn't require any great, life-changing experience. How we walk the path can quietly reveal pieces of our spiritual journey to us if we are curious and attentive.

Here are a few stories of insight and understanding that have illumined the journeys of some of my labyrinth friends.

Jo was married for nearly 25 years to a man who consistently told her that she was stupid and could do nothing right. Eventually, he had an affair with another woman he could victimize, and Jo decided to get a divorce. It was an ugly separation, and Jo worked with a therapist for a year, gaining confidence and trust in her own decisions. When I met her, we decided that a labyrinth walk might be a good way to complement her therapy.

It was a lovely sunny day out in the country where Jo took her walk to embrace a new life. I was praying for her and watching her out of the corner of my eye when she came to the end of the labyrinth and she stopped. She suddenly looked confused and then without any apparent reason, stepped over the demarcation of the labyrinth path. I called out to her, "Jo, why did you step off the path?" She said, "Did I? I got mixed-up and thought I was walking the wrong way." When she returned to the place where she'd got muddled, she realized that she was within a few steps of exiting the labyrinth. She said, "Oh, my goodness, that's what happens to me. I don't trust my own way!"

Jo and I explored that little scenario together. She didn't take her misstep as a negative message. She'd walked just about the whole labyrinth without problem—it was only at the end that her fear of claiming her own path deflected her. Jo saw how far she'd come in a year and understood that trusting her own way would need a little more practice. The labyrinth walk merely affirmed that fact. A couple of weeks later, I received a lovely invitation to join her and her friends in an anniversary party to celebrate her one-year independence.

On another occasion, I worked with a woman who hated to follow rules and directions. She liked to pursue her own way. She appreciated that there are really no rules in the labyrinth and acted on that premise. She was like watching a butterfly swooping down and alighting for a few moments, then flitting to another part of the labyrinth. She would walk for a few turns and then dart off again to whichever part of the walk appealed to her. There's nothing wrong with this, but it did illuminate this woman's antipathy towards compliance and following directions. This tendency sometimes caused her a great deal of time and energy, as she resisted the job requirements of other people's rules and had to play catch-up with courses and requirements she avoided: As in the labyrinth, so in her life.

I'm happy to say that she has reached the place and recognition in her life that she has aspired to, and as Frank Sinatra might say: She did it her way!

My editor, Chris Angermann, designed his own ritual in the labyrinth to help him heal the split identity of culture experience that all immigrants feel.

Chris came to this country from Germany when he was 12. Although he has lived in the United States for more than 40 years, he still felt the tension between his two cultures. When he took a workshop on spiritual development, which required everyone to do a final project, he devised the following ritual: He decided to do a labyrinth walk of integration. It took him a while to figure out how to do it. When his turn came up, he laid out a labyrinth on the floor of the large meeting room with golden chains Christmas decorations. At the center he placed a small altar with a display of a German and United States flags, a dish of heart-shaped chocolates and a large bowl filled with water. He invited everyone in the group to join him, explaining he would begin and end the ceremony. He played soothing music on a tape player, lit some sticks of incense, dimmed the lights, lit a candle and walked into the labyrinth. In the center, he lit a floating candle and put it in the water ball. Taking one of the chocolate hearts, he walked back out and handed the candle to the next pilgrim. One by one, the participants followed in his footsteps. Some walked slowly and carefully, concerned that the candle might go out, others moved quickly into the labyrinth. Some led with the candle, others held it by their side. Some lingered at the altar for a while before setting their candle afloat and taking a chocolate heart with them, others performed the ceremony quickly. At the end, he took the walk again, spending some time in the center looking at the twin flags and the assembly of luminescent candles floating in the bowl. Then he returned and brought the ritual to a close.

Chris later told me that he had no great revelations at the time, but everyone was moved by the quiet beauty of the ritual. The reverberations for him continued, however, like ripples traveling across a pond. As it turned out, that labyrinth walk marked the beginning of his career as a serious writer and editor, embracing English—his second language (in which he was considerably more proficient than his first)—and helping others tell their stories.

Some of my own "Aha'" moments have occurred when I introduced the labyrinth to children.

During an intergenerational session of a workshop I was holding in Northern Minnesota, the younger children ran into the labyrinth, raced round the circles and ran out again. I thought to myself, "Oh, they just had a good time; they didn't understand what they were doing." I couldn't have been more wrong! When I came back to the labyrinth an hour later, I discovered that they had gone off into the woods, picked wild flowers and decorate the center of the labyrinth.

The children taught me to be careful about making judgments too quickly and presuming that, as the expert, I always know best.

In another instance, a group of children on the Gulf Coast created a labyrinth in their school yard prior my arrival for a workshop I was going to do for them after Hurricane Katrina. The adults had told me earlier they wanted to move past Katrina and all the sadness she had brought them. They were sick of her, didn't want to speak of her, and intended the labyrinth experience to be a purposeful step forward into a better future. The children, however, knew better. When I looked at the labyrinth they had made, I saw that it consisted of the debris from Katrina—broken shells, pieces of rock, and bricks from the remains of their houses. The children knew in their hearts that past, present and future must coexist and be held in tension, and that their tragedy and sadness must be incorporated into the walk in order to move forward. They knew it deeply and intuitively, so they brought their pain as well as their hope to the building of their labyrinth.

Chapter Eleven

Modernity

Things fall apart; the centre cannot hold;
Mere anarchy is loosed upon the world.

—W.B. Yeats

"Man's life is a cheat and disappointing: All things are unreal," say the Four Tempters to Archbishop Thomas Becket in T.S. Eliot's *Murder in the Cathedral*. They insist that life has no meaning—it's all a façade, an image, an illusion. In a plugged-in electronic world of virtual reality and cyberspace with apps for every occasion, it's hard to know what is authentic and what is not. While technology has brought us miraculous and astounding gifts, it has also unbalanced us as a society. Preoccupied with image, fashion, money and celebrity, we sense that our existence is fragile and tenuous, so we hold on to material things as if for dear life. With an unstable grasp of what truly matters, it is difficult to sort out what is enduring and has integrity. The soul has a deep need to connect with what is tangible, grounded and unwavering. We are like small children who have no ability to sort out fact from fantasy and for whom the life of the imagination is as real as their concrete surroundings. But children have adults to take care of them and guide them. We'd like to think we've outgrown that developmental stage and can differentiate between what's real and what's not. For many of us, that appears to be untrue, however, and we don't know what we can rely upon.

In that regard, the ancient stories and myths once again become a treasure trove of wisdom for us. Take one of the adventures in Homer's *Odyssey*, for example. As a society, we resemble Ulysses' motley crew of mariners in the land of the Lotus Eaters who, once they tasted the intoxicating, narcotic lotus blossoms, lost their energy and purpose and became prisoners of their desire for continual sensual pleasure. It is not hard to see the parallels with our time! Addiction in various forms has become a sickness of epidemic proportions throughout Western societies. People are tuned in to their own self-gratification, and tuned out to what is actually happening around them. Most of us are not even aware that we live in a semi-drugged state—plugged in to our iPods, iPhones, computers, crackberries and TVs—as sales for mind-altering substances, anti-depressants, alcohol, uppers and downers are booming.

The post-modern world in which we find ourselves provides us with multiple images and information in quick succession. As Marshall McLuhan observed, "The medium is the message," and we are fed "sound bites"—an interesting image that describes, unintentionally no doubt, the nutritionless, Madison Avenue inspired pablum that we consume so much of in our lives. Not so long ago, people were comfortable with following complex arguments in print, or listening to longer discussions about various issues on television. Today, we prefer byte-size bits of information fed to us in quick succession. A glance at television news screens will confirm this observation. There is no longer just one picture or piece of information to absorb. There is a person talking, with a crawl line underneath featuring "breaking news." Frequently, there are as many as four split screens providing different images simultaneously to illustrate the subject.

Thomas Friedman wrote in his New York Times column of November 23, 2010, about a 14-year old girl, Allison Miller, who sends and receives a mind numbing 27,000 text messages per month. Of course, she has little time for school and other activities. As we are steeped in a world of electronic media, we experience changes in brain chemistry and patterns of information transmission. Research has confirmed that people's concentration spans have altered neurologically. Our capacity for sustained intellectual effort, serious discourse, concentration and analysis has been reduced due to our exposure to electronic media.

In his book, *The Spectacle of Worship in a Wired World: Electronic Culture and the Gathered People of God*, Tex Sample discusses the resulting culture gap that has opened. He examines how generations born post-1945 process knowledge in a different way than their forbears. They are less dependent on the written word. People are being "wired" differently in the enormous changes brought by new developments in electronic technology. These differences are not merely perceptual, but seem to be much deeper, rooted in neuro-biology and changed brain chemistry. The impact of these changes cannot be overemphasized. Sample illustrates this phenomenon in the ways he and his son approach "meaning." He wants to explain, his son wants to exclaim.

If I want to re-present in words, he wants to present in an enactment. If I want to name the dynamics of grief and loss, he wants to weep.... His search is an emotive and embodied excitement that can claim an undeniable authenticity. My approach has the "distance" of a print culture; his has the "convergence" of an electronic one.

Our young people are trapped in a world of multiple realities, and their brains have become used to constantly switching tasks, so that they are less easily able to focus and sustain attention.

Technology also makes it possible for us to assume multiple personas. As we enter virtual chat rooms, are we communicating with real people, or merely their avatars? How do we know? We have lost our way and identity in a virtual landscape. Others do not know who we are, and we are alienated from ourselves. John O'Donohue, in his book *Eternal Echoes: Celtic Reflections on Our Yearning to Belong,* describes this lonely sense of being lost, this numbness of the spirit, with laser-sharp perception:

The media present endless images of togetherness, talk shows, and parties. Yet, behind all the glossy imagery and activity, there is a haunted lonesomeness at the vacant heart of contemporary life.

People these days often express feelings of loneliness and isolation. No wonder that chat rooms, social networks, constant texting and on-line dating have gained such prominence in our lives. Never have so many communicated so much about so little and of marginal value. We are the "'richest" people in the history of the world, but we sense that something is lost, so we try to find it. But balance can't be restored entirely by therapy and counseling, and especially not by that favorite American pastime, "retail therapy," which only creates another addiction and a nation of "shopaholics." When we believe that "The one with the most toys wins," we have bought into a story of disempowerment and diminishment of our true selves.

The delectable food and treats of Lotus Land are empty of spiritual nutrition, so we are forever hungry and dissatisfied. Doctors' offices are filled with patients experiencing eating disorders. Many of them are young women, trying to exercise some control over their environment and dysfunctional lives in the way they relate to food. Obesity, with its attendant ailments and pathologies, is a national scourge as we desperately try to use food to deal with the gaping holes in our spirits.

The other enormous pressure modernity exerts is the near universal emphasis on scientific thought. If an experience is not replicable in scientific terms, it is diminished and considered irrelevant. This, despite the fact that much of our lives cannot be expressed in scientific terms. We cannot quantify the love we have for our families. We cannot measure the beauty of the Mississippi River. We cannot describe our reaction to music and drama, or the experience of joy or grief in any meaningful scientific way. Yet, these intensely human reactions connect us with the earth and with one another. They are signs or signals of our spiritual nature. Such feelings and emotional responses are a profound language, too, and we dismiss it at our peril.

Perhaps this is why an interest in pilgrimage, journey and labyrinths has developed over the last 30 years and has become important again in our consciousness. The human soul desperately desires to go on a journey to find meaning, vitality, connection and a sense of belonging. We take up the quest to resacralize our world and to find ourselves. And as we set out on the sacred journey, we hope to find others with whom to walk in companionship, whose prayers and energies will enhance our own.

On a journey, we open ourselves to physical experience and the convergence on multiple levels of images, sounds, smells, stories, and physical comfort and discomfort. We have to struggle with our resistance and what it might be revealing to us. While the physical distance may seem short on a labyrinth, the emotional, psychic, spiritual distance travelled may be immense. It is not the length of the journey that counts, it's the depths we reach on the interior walk. In addition, our discoveries allow us to reconnect with our sense of community.

Sample, in addressing the issue of how information and meaning are transmitted in a technological age, notes that the metaphor of journey and spiritual journey is very rich for Baby Boomers and Generation Xers. It is also being documented that periods of mediation, prayer and contemplation have significant effect on our brain patterns, causing us to have higher concentration and longer focus. As I have noted already, in some places, where the labyrinth is used for ADD children, such as tracing a labyrinth path with a finger at a desk before engaging in a task, it seems to help concentrate thinking and bring balance.

At the same time, pilgrimage hunger also has to do with our desire for the Holy, with the need to heal the schizoid split between the polarities of the sacred and profane. Many people are dissatisfied with the answers provided by professional religious leaders because they attempt to nourish soul hunger with talk alone, ignoring the need for sacred connection with the earth and their bodies. As a result, a growing number of men and women are no longer willing to rely on the religious "experts" for their spiritual growth. We have become very skilled at getting our own needs met, and all too often institutional religion and churches—locked in a patriarchal, hierarchical model—have not adapted to the spiritual cries of their parishioners . The priest/pastor/rabbi/imam has an important role as guardian of the Holy, but people need to experience more than just listening to the dogmatic views and inclinations of their official leaders. This is a change that hopefully will push ordained ministers of all denominations to deepen their sensitivities and begin to seek new ways to develop word, ritual and worship.

Walking the labyrinth and going on pilgrimage may not be the ultimate solution, but they are ways of finding our true identities and giving us the courage to bring our real, authentic presence to our situation. Such presence is desperately needed, because it allows us to tell the truth about what is happening and to draw boundaries in a way that is health producing and life affirming.

If the center cannot hold and we seem to be spiraling out of control, as Yeats' poem suggests, what better way to restore cohesion than by walking in circumscribed circles, circles that do not lose their center, circles that hold energy in the bounded structure of their design and construction. Sacred space, sacred travel and prayer help us to discern where the limits need to be in our lives, and so we return to the circles of the labyrinth to embark on an exterior and interior journey: We return to walking to discover our true selves and then offer that self to the blessing of the world.

Chapter Twelve

To Bless the World

They cannot scare me with their empty spaces
Between stars—on stars where no human race is.
I have it in me so much nearer home
To scare myself with my own desert places.

—Robert Frost

The picture of the earth viewed from space, a blue orb, brilliant and beautiful against the stark blackness of outer space, is still at work shaping our consciousness about all of us belonging together. A child asked after seeing the image on a poster, "Where are the country lines?" She had only seen the earth portrayed in an atlas with the borders of nations demarcated in outline. The idea of all of us and the whole order of creatures existing within the confines of this sphere, the earth, is still in its infancy. We rotate in space with nothingness surrounding us. Our earth literally has no solid underpinnings. We are kept in place by complex gravitational energies and unseen forces over which we have no control. The planets of the solar system orbit the sun, each separated from the other by vast distances yet held together by an invisible, powerful web of attraction and relationship.

That is the macro image of the cosmos in which we live. If we journey inwards to the micro level, we discover a mirror image of the pattern of our circling planetary systems. We see electrons orbiting the nucleus of the atom. What appears to us as dense matter is in fact composed of minute whirling units of energy separated from each other, but held together in relationship. Our working concept of what is solid, concrete and reliable, while necessary for everyday living, is limited. The mystics have always understood this truth, now we know it scientifically.

As a part of this incredible mystery of circling energy, we sense our vulnerability, so some of us take to walking in circles intentionally, because—whether in a formal labyrinth or not —the form of the circle is engrained in our spirits and is part of our being. Monks circumambulate their sacred shrines, in Ireland pilgrims make *turas* (which means "journey" in Gaelic) around sacred wells and cairns, Muslims circle the Ka'ba in Mecca, and in Nepal, prayer wheels line holy paths, which passersby spin on their pilgrimages.

In our dawning awareness of what it might mean to be a global community, we are beginning to appreciate that the Butterfly Effect—sensitive dependence on initial conditons— is not just about the systems of nature, but is reflected in our own lives and in society. The concept derives its colorful name from the observation that actions as infinitesimal as the flapping of a butterfly's wings in one corner of the globe can affect far away weather patterns. Tiny changes in one place can lead to big changes in another. What we do has consequences, although we have known it only abstractly.

A seemingly insignificant walk in a circle or praying in one place can have consequences and affect life in another!

We are just beginning to realize our interdependence. A virus from a Chinese chicken can cause a global outbreak of bird flu. Our military, returning from violent conflicts and to the families they have been separated from, face serious problems. Suicide rates among servicemen and women are climbing steeply. Anger, addiction and Post-Traumatic Stress Disorder (PTSD) may all be part of the duffle bag contents veterans carry home with them. How this baggage will affect us and our society remains to be seen, but we can be sure that it will have a powerful influence.

How do we respond? The labyrinth is not a cure-all! But it does offer a beginning, helping us get in touch with the difficulties that beset us and giving us courage to face them. It is also an extraordinary path of healing and peace that can be very well combined with conventional therapy because of its inclusive, sacramental, symbolic nature. It can provide a natural interface between veterans' organizations and communities that want to go beyond the "yellow ribbon" welcome and give returnees and their family members support that is heartfelt soul care.

In some sense, it might be true to say that the labyrinth has chosen us, after centuries of forgetfulness and neglect, to rise to the surface and offer its gracious healing presence at a time when our consciousness is in need of revitalization. But, while labyrinths are being built across the world, much more attention must be given to training people in their use. We who are interested in labyrinths must train not only individuals but groups of people on the role of the labyrinth as healing space, and design rituals for use in the context of the walker's story.

Otherwise these powerful circles will once more be forgotten and sink back into obscurity.

Here is a concrete example of what I mean: The Rev. Kerry Holder-Joffrion and I were hosts together with the Church of the Nativity in Huntsville, Alabama, for a group of leaders from St. Paul's Chapel, New York, who work in hospitality and reconciliation. They had come to experience pilgrimage with us, because they host over 2.5 million visitors/pilgrims annually. Their tiny chapel, which suffered little damage during 9/11, was the primary place of rest, recuperation and spiritual strength for the workers in the pit of hell at Ground Zero. It became the headquarters for healing and grace for all who were working in the ruins. The visitors still come, I think, not only to see the site for themselves, but also to experience a place where hope blossomed in a dark time, where love was expressed in action, and where the spirit of holy kindness overcame a grotesque attack of hatred and evil. There is a sense that, at that chapel and in the location of those ruined twin towers, so much intensity of care took place, some of that blessing continues to radiate; and the visitors want to participate in the blessing.

The members of the group that came to see us in Alabama wanted to feel for themselves what it was like to be a pilgrim, not just a host to pilgrims. While we took them on the Jonathan Daniels, Martyrs of Alabama Pilgrimage, an important local Civil Rights pilgrimage, we also asked them to walk a labyrinth with us.

Our pilgrims told us that many of the first responders on September 11 took off their shoes and tied them to the railings of the chapel garden before putting on their work boots and running into the doomed twin towers. The shoes remained tied there for a long time as a physical reminder of the extreme sacrifice made by their owners and became one of the symbols that marked that terrible day. One member of the group of St. Paul's pilgrims had lost her shoes, too, that day in the surreal cloud of dust, ash and fear that swept over lower Manhattan. She had walked home nearly 15 miles on bare feet. As we listened to her account and thought about how to make the event most beneficial for the group, we realized that fire had been a crucial part of their experience, so we placed flaming torches around the beautiful labyrinth on Monte Sano Mountain, pictured on the cover of this book, because the cosmic element that had caused the destruction must also be reclaimed in blessing. Along the curving path they would walk, we placed old shoes to help them remember their story of the shoes and see that the path of pain is, paradoxically, also the fire walk of grace. Following their walk in the labyrinth, under the blazing stars of an Alabama night sky, they were anointed with the oil of healing and blessing. They left the labyrinth in silence.

The St. Paul's Chapel leaders went home and discussed with their congregation what had happened on their pilgrimage. Together they decided to have a labyrinth made for their sacred space to expand their healing and blessing work. In addition to regular labyrinth uses throughout the year, on the eve of September 11, St. Paul's Chapel holds an all night vigil of prayer and labyrinth walks for the peace of the world.

In considering how to best invite people of all backgrounds into labyrinth use, one place to look is the Hallmark Company's catalogue of significant events. It points the way by identifying the holidays, seasons and events that the public now marks by sending a card. These anniversaries and celebrations all carry powerful associations and complex emotions for us that can be brought to a labyrinth walk. Valentine's Day, Mother's Day, Father's Day, Veterans Day, Thanksgiving, religious festivals, graduations, births and deaths are events whose experience can be heightened in a sacred space. The Rev. Diana Wheeler decorated a labyrinth with glowing pumpkins one year and placed a bowl of treats in the middle. The children who had to walk through scary trees, flickering shadows and cobwebs until they reached the labyrinth, were treated to a lighted pumpkin path leading to candy treasure. A German tradition in a lovely variation on the Scandinavian festival of St. Lucia—where on December 13 a little girl with a crown of lights leads a candlelight procession—makes use of the Christmas festival. Children are invited to walk as sacred light bearers, carrying candles into a labyrinth decorated with evergreen branches. Participants in this ritual will never forget it. What a lovely way to honor the season and bless the future.

Many non-conventional weddings now take place on a labyrinth, celebrating the union of two people in a sacred space. I have already mentioned that the labyrinth is a powerful container for grief and rage, as demonstrated by the request for its use on the streets of the Castro in San Francisco following a shooting. Hospitals and birthing centers are natural places for labyrinth use. Spiritual care departments in hospitals are paying attention to the labyrinth, but the work can go much further and deeper. The occasions are ready-made for us; what ritual we will create is limited only by our imaginations.

As you consider how to invite others to walk your labyrinth, important questions to ask are: How much control do you demand over the use of the labyrinth? How will you invite people into this sacred space without demanding conformity and compliance with your own particular set of beliefs? Can you allow other people to embrace the holy and trust the labyrinth walk itself to be the medium of transformation? And finally, how will you expand its use?

As we walk the way of the labyrinth, we gain the courage and energy not only to receive blessing, but to be blessings. In our 21st-century world, there is no more important work than becoming conscious of what is destructive and what is healing and life giving for ourselves and our planet. It is time to seize Ariadne's golden thread and walk into the center of our global, social and individual pain in order to be reborn and find out who we really are. It is time to take the journey of self-discovery, to go on pilgrimage, to walk the labyrinth. It is time to be the soul friend, the *anamchara,* of those who need a companion on the Way.

These words are written in the hope that many will be inspired to leave their safe and ordinary cocoons, to let go of certainty and crippling ideologies, tie their everyday shoes to the railing, and strap on their work boots to walk together with others into new and deeper relationships for the healing of the world. We walk for our own becoming and for the blessing of all creation: We walk for the resacralization of our relationship with our planet and ourselves.

Petroglyph labyrinth

Works Cited

Eliade, M. (1987). *The Sacred & The Profane: The Nature of Religion.* NY: Harcourt Brace.

Fox, M. (1997). *Natural Grace: Dialogues on Creation, Darkness, and the Soul in Spirituality and Science.* NY: Image Books.

Johnson, R.A. (1991). *Owning Your Own Shadow: Understanding the Dark Side of the Psyche.* San Francisco: Harper.

Kermeen, M. (n.d.). "Labyrinths in Stone." Retrieved from http://www.labyrinthbuilder.com/

McCullough, D.W. (2005). *The Unending Mystery: A Journey Through Labyrinths & Mazes.* Anchor Books.

O'Donohue, J. (1999). *Eternal Echoes.* NY: HarperCollins.

O'Donohue, J. (2008). *To Bless the Space Between Us: A Book of Blessings.* NY: DoubleDay.

Quammen, D. (2010, November). "Mysteries of Great Migrations." National Geographic, pp. 37-51.

Sacks, J. R. (2005). *To Heal a Fractured World: The Ethics of Responsibility.* NY: Schocken Books.

Sample, T. (1998). *The Spectacle of Worship in a Wired World: Electronic Culture and the Gathered People of God.* Nashville: Abingdon Press.

Bibliography

This is a very brief bibliography of the labyrinth, but these titles are a good place to begin.

Artress, Lauren. *Walking a Sacred Path: Rediscovering the Labyrinth as a Spiritual Tool.* Riverhead Books, 1996.

Artress, Lauren. *The Sand Labyrinth: Meditation at your fingertips.* Charles Tuttle Co. 2000.

Artress, Lauren. *The Sacred Path Companion: A Guide to Walking the Labyrinth to Heal & Transform.* The Penguin Group. 2006.

Conty, Patrick & Arianne. T*he Genesis and Geometry of the Labyrinth: Architecture, Hidden Language, Myths and Rituals.* Inner Traditions International Ltd., 2002.

Cousineau, Phil. *The Art of Pilgrimage: The Seeker's Guide to Making Travel Sacred.* Conari Press. 1998.

Curry, Helen. *The Way of the Labyrinth: A Powerful Meditation for Everyday Life.* Penguin, 2003.

Gayle West, Melissa A. *Exploring the Labyrinth: A Guide for Healing.* Broadway, 2000.

Kern, Hermann. *Through the Labyrinth: Designs and Meaning over 5000 Years.* Prestel, Munich, 2000.

Kimberly Hartwell Geoffrion, Jill. *Living the Labyrinth: 101 Paths to a Deeper Connection with the Sacred*. Pilgrim Press, 2001

Kimberly Hartwell Geoffrion, Jill, Lauren Artress. *Praying the Labyrinth: A Journal for Spiritual Exploration*. Pilgrim Press 1999.

Kimberly Hartwell Geoffrion, Jill. *The Labyrinth and the Song of Songs*. Pilgrim Press, 2003.

Raphael Sands, Helen, Robert Ferre. *The Healing Labyrinth: Finding Your Path to Inner Peace*. Barrons Educational Service, 2001.

You may contact Zara Renander at

jzrenander@gmail.com
or
www.turningpointconsultants.com